D1523198

the boy's book of
Backyard Camping

the boy's book of
Backyard
Camping

Allan A. Macfarlan

GALAHAD BOOKS • NEW YORK CITY

Published by Galahad Books, a division of A & W Pro-
motional Book Corporation, 95 Madison Avenue, New
York, N.Y. 10016, by arrangement with Stackpole Books,
Cameron and Kelker Streets, Harrisburg, Pa. 17105.

Library of Congress Catalog Card No. 73-81647
ISBN: 0-88365-027-4

Manufactured in the United States of America.

contents

maps, and landmarks • how to make tree blazes without harming trees • what first aid treatments to administer for blisters, bruises, burns, cuts, insect bites, poison ivy infection, and sprains • what to include in a practical, compact first aid kit • which antiseptics are best

• tells how to make three different types of shelter-tent • how to make versatile cooking utensils from shortening cans and aluminum foil • easy ways to improvise grates, pot hooks, toasting forks, wash basin stands, and windbreaks • how to give your camp a personality all its own by decorating it with homemade pennants and trail signs

• tells where to find bargains in camp equipment • how not to get stuck with gear you don't like • how to choose comfortable clothing • what materials are needed to keep clothes in good repair • how to care for tents between camping seasons • how to avoid losing important items • why it is important to choose useful, rather than flashy, equipment • which axes and saws to buy and what they are good for • about common-sense safety rules for handling axes and knives like a seasoned camper • what tools every camp should have

• tells how to make time fly by playing exciting games requiring minimal equipment • about games that test agility, balance, and compass-reading skills • about wit-sharpening games requiring shrewd detection and clever deception

• tells how to set up a backyard camping show and how to attract an audience • what materials to use in making model tents, tepees, logs, and campfires • how to impress parents and friends with displays of skill in knot-tying and making your own gadgets • what the duties of the master of ceremonies are • about audience-stumping quizzes and riddles together with their answers

THE BOY'S BOOK OF BACKYARD CAMPING

A Word About Backyard Camping

LOTS OF people today are saying that modern civilization has made American boys soft. They are wrong. The American boy today has the same desire his hardy forebears had to face the elements and win. The place where he can learn to do this is in his own backyard.

Quite a few of the world's great explorers learned many of their survival skills in a backyard camp. So can boys today.

By mastering basic camping skills in his own backyard, a boy learns to be self-reliant and gains confidence in his own abilities. This self-respect, in turn, wins him respect not only from boys his own age, but from grownups as well.

Adults are quite willing to listen to a boy who knows what he is talking about. Practicing camping skills in a backyard or neighborhood camp makes a boy look like an old hand in the outdoors, even on outings in rugged country. An expert backyard camper will be able to act as technical adviser to his family, if it should decide to go on a camping trip. Such a boy will be able and ready to do his share as a member of any camping group, whether it pitches its tents in the wilderness or in a municipal park.

A skilled backyard camper is able to hold up his end in any enterprise. He can think quickly and act fast in emergencies. Like the American pioneers, he can make do with little equipment and often make his own. He is a good member to have on any team.

Many boys across the country are not only learning how to rough it in backyard camps, but also enjoying the adventure of camping under the stars. Why not join them?

1. BECOMING A

SEASONED CAMPER in your own backyard

BOYS TODAY are lucky. They need not start from scratch as they learn the principles of good camping. Their cavemen ancestors were not so fortunate, however.

Cavemen Campers

These primitive, hardy, early ancestors of ours learned to camp the hard way, by trial and error. There were no records left by earlier campers to warn them not to choose a home in a cave which would be under water as soon as floods rushed through the gorges. There were no books to tell them not to leave a second entry into the cave through which a bear or saber-toothed tiger could enter. When a family was raided by such fierce animals, often one member managed to escape. The survivor warned others to sleep in a cave with only one entry, blocked at night by rocks or stones, or else to block all openings large enough to admit unwelcome visitors.

PRIMITIVE SHELTERS Driven by circumstances, necessity, curiosity, or the urge for adventure, these early campers graduated from caves to various other kinds of shelter. They slept under ledges of low-hung cliffs and outcroppings of rock. When they chose solid cliffs, with ledges projecting far enough to protect them from storm and rain, their temporary shelters became home.

The more nomadic of these early campers, who had no family ties and felt the urge to explore, went farther afield. They slept in trees, under low-hanging branches, or behind low screens of thick bushes, learning by trial and error to camp on the side away from the wind. Such primitive shelters were crude and seldom dry.

These early outdoorsmen devised much better shelters as their intelligence developed. They gradually learned to build crude huts and even comfortable lake dwellings, raised on stilts, as protection from rising waters and floods, which had wiped out so many of their ancestors.

Countless centuries have passed since primitive days. During all this time, bigger and better brains have concentrated on the varied problems of comfortable outdoor living. Despite this, man is still spending endless hours and countless dollars, designing better, more efficient camping equipment. And all this improved equipment is at the service of today's backyard camper.

Learning Outdoor Skills in a Backyard Camp

Not only do modern boys have the advantage of better camping equipment, but they can also practice basic camping skills under ideal conditions.

There is much evidence which proves that a backyard camp is the best place to learn many camping skills. Several boys, whose only knowledge of knots was acquired in their backyard camps, have won first prizes in keen, competitive knot-tying contests. Many boys who concentrated on first aid in their own backyards have developed considerable skill in applying triangular bandages. In fact, doctors have made use of their knowledge and services when instructing classes of adults who were candidates for first aid certificates.

TEAMING UP   Boys often learn camping skills better by teaming up. What better way can a boy test his progress as a camper than by matching his skills against other boys his own age?

Each boy in a small group of backyard campers might have his own camp and take turns visiting the others' camps.

The boys can use the biggest backyard for working together on various campcraft and gadgetry projects. There is also no reason why a lone camper should not invite several friends over to his yard. He and his friends might eventually form a small camping club. There may be a recreation center or play lot in the neighborhood which the club can arrange to use for camping activities.

Many of the camping activities in this book are suitable for small groups of boys. But whether a boy camps alone or with a few pals, he will find backyard camping an exciting adventure.

2. KNOWING

ALL
about
tents

IT IS HARD to imagine camping anywhere without a tent. Since early times, many of the world's most adventurous people—nomadic tribesmen, cowboys, prospectors, and intrepid explorers—have lived in tents.

When you are planning to set up camp in the backyard, you will probably decide first of all what kind of tent to use. There is a wide selection of tents on the market today, but you need not restrict your choice to the ready-made tents. A backyard camper without too much money to spend might very well decide to make his own shelter. See Chapter 6 for directions on how to make your own tents.

A good tent is fairly expensive, but if you can save up money to buy one, it may prove money well spent—when you are certain what kind of tent you want. A good-quality tent should give good service for six to ten years and perhaps considerably longer, especially when it is used for only two or three months each year. (See Chapter 7 for tips on tent care.)

Pup and similar small tents for one or two boys vary in price from about $5 to $15. Medium-weight, standard model tents, accommodating one to four boys, range in price from $15 to $40. Special lightweight backpacking tents, with space for one to four boys, sell from $32 up to $140. The cheaper tents in this price range have an approximate floor measurement of six by four feet and a height of about three feet six inches. The more expensive models have a floor measurement of about seven by ten feet and a height of five or six feet.

Although many tents are the same size and look alike, their prices differ. The price of a tent is determined by the material of which it is made, its weight, and how well it is sewn and finished.

Never buy a tent sewn together with the chain stitch. In

the chain stitch only one thread is used. The stitches are looped in a chainlike way and if even one stitch breaks, the whole chain of stitches will work loose. If possible, buy a tent sewn together with the lock stitch. This is a method of sewing in which two threads are interlocked. The lock stitch does not come undone easily. (These remarks about stitching also apply to the packs discussed in Chapter 7.) Rustless fittings are also desirable in a tent, but add to its cost.

Not only should you beware of shoddily made tents, but you should also avoid buying a tent that is too well constructed for your needs. Many tents are manufactured to meet the demands of wealthy campers. Others are designed for mountaineering or exploring expeditions, which require feather-light tents capable of defying gales and terrific strain. The tents described in this chapter are the more practical and serviceable ones, sold at reasonable prices.

Because the fabric *is* the tent, it is well to note the materials of which tents are made. Really lightweight tents are no longer made of canvas, cotton, drill, or duck, but of one of the modern lightweight, weatherproof fabrics which have recently been discovered.

Waterproofing vs. Weatherproofing

Tents should never be made from waterproof material. To be healthy and dry inside, tents must breathe. Waterproof materials, being non-porous, cannot breathe. Water-repellent or weatherproof fabrics, made water-resistant by various treatments, will not only repel moisture and rain but also admit air and keep healthfully dry inside. Some inexpensive, treated types of cotton, canvas, poplin, and drill are weatherproof and give good service.

Featured among the fine but more expensive modern

fabrics are various treated nylons, dacrons, and pima cotton materials. Still newer fabrics are being tested and treated.

WATERPROOF FLIES   For campers who do not trust the cheaper weatherproof fabrics to give protection in heavy rain, a completely waterproof fly is a sure-fire remedy. Such a fly, rigged about a foot above the tent roof and extending twelve to eighteen inches beyond each side of the tent, assures complete protection against the heaviest rain. The fly may be suspended over the tent roof on a rope attached to two poles, one at each end of the tent. Of course, these two poles must be supported by guy ropes pegged to the ground. To give additional support, lash one of the poles with a clove hitch, near the top and at the foot, to the tent pole at the front of the tent. A rope can be attached to each corner of a tent fly, preferably with the clove hitch (see Chapter 5). The clove hitch can also be used to fasten the other end of the rope to the tent peg. Some tents come equipped with flies and have poles to support both tent and fly.

A fly need not be made of coated nylon or any expensive material. It can be a tarp made of strong lightweight plastic or canvas which can stand sun as well as heavy downpours. Such flies make the insides of tents cool, but opaque tarps can make tents too dark. Stout transparent plastic tarps will not darken tents too much.

What Color Tent?

The diffused sunlight streaming into a tent is one of the joys of camping, so dark-colored, opaque material is not a real camper's choice. Morning sunlight filtering through a pale orange or buttercup-yellow fabric is a delight. The early morning sun shining through a light tan, pale green, or cream-colored material is also cheerful. The chief disadvantage of a white tent is that it soils easily, unless great care is taken of it until it "weathers" with time.

Red, orange, or black tents are good for snow-covered terrain. A brightly colored tent is easy to spot on a sandy shore or desert. These considerations should be kept in mind, if such sites are accessible to a camping boy and/or his family.

Families usually prefer colorful, pretty tents, and there are tents of all colors and shades on the market to satisfy them. On organized campgrounds, tents of all colors and multicolors abound.

Pitching a Tent

The first thing to think of when pitching a tent is choosing the best location. Naturally, the backyard camper does not have an unlimited choice of tentsites. Nevertheless, he may have some choice in deciding where to pitch his tent. The following considerations apply to picking tentsites in backyards and play lots, as well as in wilderness areas.

A tent should be pitched on fairly smooth ground. No hollow should be under the tent or next to it. It is best to face a tent towards the southeast whenever possible, because such an exposure assures the warmth of early morning sunlight. Erecting a tent on slightly sloping, porous soil will provide good drainage and avoid the necessity of ditching.

It is best not to ditch a tent at all. Furthermore, a boy's parents may have serious objections to his digging up the turf in their backyard. However, if your tent must be ditched, ditch only on its two sides and rear, so that the water is drained toward the lowest ground. Dig a shallow, narrow trench, not cut in the form of a "V," about four inches deep and three inches wide, just outside the tent walls where the rain run-off falls. The earth taken from the ditch should be carefully carried away from the tent area. Never pile it alongside the tent walls.

Allow plenty of time to set up your camp. In a backyard, allow at least three hours of daylight to work in. (If you were working on primitive terrain or an unorganized site, setting up camp would take at least half a day.) When several boys camp together, different suitable jobs should be assigned to each. Two or three can pitch the tent, while another two or three can arrange the kitchen and dining area.

TENT POLES, PEGS, AND MECHANISMS   Backyard campers need not feel that they are making too many concessions to civilization when they buy their tent poles and pegs from camp outfitters rather than cut down saplings and hack off branches to make their own. It should be obvious to most boys that such a method of making tent poles and pegs would be highly destructive of their parents' property. Even on organized public and private campgrounds, the cutting of saplings is usually forbidden. In tree-covered, primitive territory, suitable straight poles are very hard to locate. It obviously does not make sense to cut down useful saplings to make useless tent poles.

Although many modern tents have metal suspension frames and other novelty gadgets for holding a tent up, regular tent poles of lightweight wood or metal still continue to play their part in camping. Lightweight wooden poles cut into sections and joined by sticking one piece into a metal sleeve on the other, are still used by many campers. They are fairly easy to transport. Lightweight metal poles are also excellent. Those which telescope take up very little room and serve well.

CAUTION: When aluminum or other lightweight telescopic tent poles are used and nested one inside the other, for transport, the greatest care must be taken to avoid denting them. Once the outside pole is dented, it is very difficult to separate the poles.

Look out for sand, too, especially fine sand! Sand inside hollow metal tent poles or in the mechanism of a pop-up tent causes real trouble. Pop-up tents will not pop, nor will metal poles come apart or telescope. During transport, the ends of the poles should be protected by a cloth or canvas wrapping. The poles should never be left lying on the ground. The parts of modern tents which open mechanically should also be protected until the frame is in place, ready to be opened.

Campers should beware of some insufficiently field-tested trick tents, some of which are supposed to almost pitch themselves. When they work smoothly, they can be wonderful. However, when they fail to function in an unexpected rainstorm—through a little sand getting into the mechanism or some sudden mechanical quirk—one is inclined to say harsh things about both the inventor and the manufacturer!

Though it is not too difficult to improvise wooden tent pegs, it is usually best to have a supply of aluminum or other lightweight metal alloy tent pegs. Most of these tent pegs fit one inside the other. They range in length from about seven to fifteen inches, or longer for difficult terrain such as desert or beach. Alpine, 7-inch, metal, skewer-type tent pegs are very light and easy to pack. They will hold down the side walls of even big tents. Featherweight plastic tent pegs seven inches long with hook and skewer-type tops are also available.

Types of Tents

A backyard camper who has learned his campcraft well will sometimes be asked questions about camping by those who know little or nothing about it. For that reason, these pages discuss not only tents for lone campers, but also shelters for groups of two or three friends or the whole family. You can become technical adviser to your family, if they decide to join the millions of campers experiencing the joys of outdoor living under canvas.

A boy should ask himself these questions when choosing a tent: How many will use it at the same time? How much room is desired? If the campsite is in a playground or park some distance from home, he should also consider how the tent will be transported.

There are a number of practical tents suitable for lone campers. These tents have lightweight fabric and lightweight framework or poles. Some of them have sewn-in floors and screened doors for protection against mosquitoes and other insects.

PUP TENT A small, wedge-shaped pup tent, without headroom or walls, offers little comfort or space, though it gives protection from weather. It can be used by a lone camper or for storage purposes. Improvised walls can be made by carefully sewing brass rings about twelve inches apart and approximately twelve inches from the foot of the canvas along each side of the tent. Guy ropes, fastened to these rings and staked to the ground, will make a pup tent a little more roomy inside. However, they will reduce the height of the tent somewhat. A ground cloth is usually used in a pup tent.

MINER'S TENT Though this is not a very good-looking tent, it has some points in its favor. It can be pitched easily on various sorts of terrain. It needs no center pole. You can use a conveniently located, safe branch for support. Just stake down the four corners of the tent and hitch a length of stout rope to the tent peak. Then throw the free end of the rope over a handy branch and pull the tent up until it is in position. Finally, drive in the stakes and make fast the free end of the rope to a tree trunk, tough bush, or tent peg. An outside flap covers the door in the modern models of this tent.

WALL TENT   Many small wall tents accommodate two boys nicely. Some can sleep three boys comfortably. Of course, most of these models can be had in various sizes.

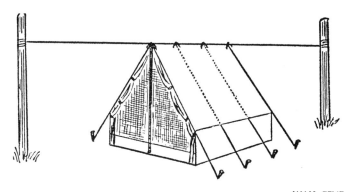

WALL TENT

The small, lightweight wall tent pictured here assures dry sleeping and real comfort. It has two-foot walls which provide elbow room, a sewn-in floor, a front flap which snaps tight, and an ample mosquito net which zips tight over the doorway. There is a mosquito-screened window at the back, with a big enough flap to lower when it rains to guarantee a dry tent.

Wall tents also come in family models which offer a maximum of usable inside space, sleeping comfort, and headroom. Single poles at each end of a family-type wall tent do not get in the way. The height of the walls ranges from around two feet to six feet. The roof slant allows adequate rain run-off. The walls assure easy ventilation, since they may be rolled up all around when desired.

Some modern wall tents have screened windows and doors, sewn-in floors, and air scoops for ventilation—luxuries which older models never had. A sewn-in sod cloth and a removable, waterproof ground cloth, available in some wall tents, make it easier to keep the floors clean.

Wall tents come in many sizes, such as 7' x 7', 8' x 10', 10' x 12', and 12' x 14'. When weight is not important, various weights of duck, ranging from eight to twelve ounces, are popular and inexpensive.

EXPLORER TENT   This is a fine, handy tent, suitable for one or two campers. It can be easily rigged to attach to trees or mount on shear poles. The big flap in front can serve as a porch in good weather and the steep wall slope sheds rain well. The cruiser tent is very similar.

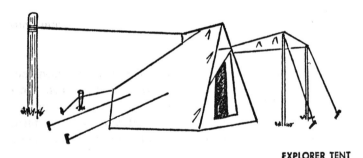

EXPLORER TENT

BAKER TENT   The baker tent also accommodates two campers. This fine tent has an open front, a slanting roof and rear wall and, often, a sewn-in floor. It is a good tent for summer use, when one wants a tent with an unobstructed view. The full-sized tent flap completely covers the front, in case of rain. It can also be used as a porch in sunny weather.

POP-UP AND DRAW-TITE TENTS   These two-man tents are lightweight, mobile, and easy and quick to set up. The pop-up has the framework inside the tent, whereas the "Draw-Tite" is suspended on a frame, giving maximum inside tent space. Both tents have frameworks made of aluminum alloys or other strong but lightweight metal.

These tents are sometimes known by different names, but they are easy to recognize. Both are good buys, though they are somewhat more expensive than simple two-man models. These tents also come in larger sizes.

FAMILY CAMPER TENT   Family-type tents such as the family camper are big and roomy. However, they are heavy, harder to pitch than smaller tents, and more likely to blow down in a windstorm. The family camper can sleep six adults with fair comfort.

UMBRELLA TENT   The umbrella tent is also popular with families in the United States. Its lack of center poles provides maximum floor space. It is either mounted on a metal suspension frame or has a corner pole assembly. Only experienced campers realize how much useful space a center pole occupies and how much it seems to get in one's way.

MULTIPLE-ROOM TENT   Some American tent manufacturers are turning out serviceable family tents with side rooms, suitable for longer stays in the open. Such tents are best used on private campsites with plenty of room for big tents.

SMALL TENTS FOR LARGE FAMILIES This idea may appear strange but, actually, it describes a happy way to assure comfortable camping with a large family. Two or three small tents weigh little more than one big tent, and provide much more floor space. In addition, they assure more privacy for each member of the family. Needless to say, smaller tents have none of the disadvantages of the larger family tents mentioned above.

Happy tenting!

3. EATING

WELL
on your
own

SOMEHOW FOOD eaten outdoors seems to taste better. This chapter tells how you can fix simple but hearty outdoor meals that will have parents, friends, and any visitors in your camp coming back for seconds.

The eating area can easily be the most popular place in camp. It may be convenient to eat near, but not too near, the "kitchen" (the stove, cook fire, or fireplace). When you have a choice, an area under a shady tree is fine. Of course, it should be upwind of the cook fire, if there is any. In case of rain, the dining area can be covered with a plastic or tarp fly suspended from trees or mounted on poles.

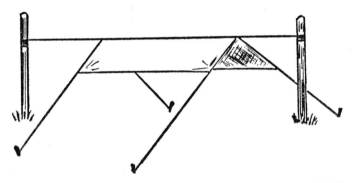

FLY FOR COVERING THE DINING AREA

A folding table and a folding bench or two or three folding chairs make a suitable outdoor dining room. If any camping or household supplies have been delivered in a fairly large wooden crate or box, it can be easily converted into a serving table-cupboard.

When such conveniences are not available, it is easy to improvise other arrangements. A ground cloth can be used as a table, and pieces of oilcloth, plastic, or tarp spread on the ground can substitute for chairs. You can place a few flat stones together to make a table, or let each camper use a stone as his personal table, if a group of boys is camping together. If there is a fireplace in the backyard, its sides may serve as a table.

A piece of waterproof cloth or plastic, spread on the ground and convenient to the cook fire, can provide working space for the cook. In sunny or rainy weather, it is a good idea to stretch a tarp or plastic fly over the cook fire and as much of the "kitchen" as possible.

Few places are more suitable for learning to build both campfires and cook fires than a backyard camp. Even if fire regulations in your neighborhood forbid the lighting of wood fires in backyards, you can learn to build fires by using artificial logs, described in Chapter 9. It is not even necessary to put a match to such fires. If you practice the fire-building methods described in this chapter, you will know how to light fires that burn real logs, and you will be able to start them easily anyplace where such fires are permitted.

Fire Safety

The first thing to do before lighting any campfire anywhere, even in your own backyard, is find out whether permission is needed. So much damage has been done to forests and woodlands by fire, that today an official fire permit is required practically everywhere that a fire can be lit outdoors. Such a permit clearly states where you may light a fire. You should also find out any regulations regarding camp cook stoves and charcoal grills.

Be sure, before lighting any fire, that you know how to control it and how to extinguish it thoroughly. Many unwanted fires which cause great damage to people, wildlife, and property are started through ignorance and carelessness. A new camper may light a little fire which gets away from him. Unless he uses his head and works very quickly, or someone comes to help him, a big, destructive fire is soon blazing fiercely.

FIRE-LIGHTING RULES Destructive runaway fires can be prevented by following the rules of safe fire-lighting and fire control. Novice campers should study these rules.

- Never light a fire near a brush pile, underbrush, or dry grass.
- Never light a fire below a tree with dead leaves and branches.
- Never light a fire against a log, stump, tree, wall, or building.
- Never light a fire on ground that has not been cleared of materials which will burn.
- Never leave a fire unattended, even for a few minutes.
- Always clear a space about six to eight feet in diameter for the fire by removing sticks, leaves, humus, and roots and scraping earth away down to mineral soil.
- Always place the fire foundation in the center of the cleared circle.
- Always throw a match used to light a fire into the fire bed. When a match has been used outdoors for any other purpose, blow it out. Then break it in two, holding each end, before throwing it onto *bare* ground.
- Always keep a bucket of water, sand, or earth handy, just in case. A broom and several heavy sacks make good fire beaters.
- Always make certain the fire is dead out before leaving it.

PUTTING OUT YOUR FIRE Even experienced campers have started big blazes by leaving a campfire or cook fire which they believed was completely out. Hours later, some hot ashes or cinders blazed up when a wind arose and carried the sparks to dry grass or brushwood nearby. Soon a big fire was raging.

Here is how to make sure a fire is really out. Carefully separate the burning and smoldering branches and embers with a green stick or metal rod. Then sprinkle water liberally all over the wood, embers, ashes, and fire bed, until absolutely certain that all smoldering material is dead out. Wait a few minutes, watching carefully. Then pour more water onto the fire bed and wherever there is even a wisp of smoke. After this, test the remains of the dead fire with your bare hands, as a sure proof that the fire has been extinguished.

When putting out a fire, never pour water directly onto a stone or brick fireplace when it is still very hot. This may crack the stones or bricks. First spread the red embers and burning sticks and branches over the grate. Then partially extinguish them with a stick to cool them down before putting the water on to complete the job.

Starting a Fire

What a fire needs most of all is air. When air is shut off from a beginning fire in any way, the fire is smothered and will not light. When starting a fire, therefore, never place heavy sticks on it.

TINDER Experienced campers prefer to use only wildwood materials to start a fire. Some which assure instant flame are dry evergreen needles, dry cedar bark, dry grass or moss, dry fuzz from pussy willows, and the dried down from milkweed or fireweed. Do not ruin beautiful birch trees by stripping off bark. Birch bark should only be taken from dead trees. It burns equally well whether wet or dry.

Of course, wildwood tinder may be hard to find in a backyard. You can solve this problem by using store-bought tinder. Or use a few candle stubs, short lengths of heavy string or cord soaked in liquid paraffin wax and then dried, or a sheet of newspaper soaked in paraffin wax, rolled up tight, and cut into two-inch lengths. All of these are effective and prove very helpful in rainy weather to inexperienced campers who want to get a fire started as quickly as possible.

KINDLING Because of the pitch in them, chips from a dead, dry pine and the roots of most dead pines, as well, make excellent kindling. Even in wet weather, the small, dry, dead branches found within arm's reach on live pines are fine for kindling. These little branches, broken from the trees, are drier than those found on the ground. If dead branches break easily with a sharp snap, they are good kindling. Live branches or trees should never be cut for fire-making.

Most other dead, thin, dry branches will also start a fire, once the tinder is laid. If such branches are not to be found in a boy's backyard, he will have to scout around for other material. Wood shavings from his father's workshop will make very good kindling.

FIREWOOD Tinder and kindling is of little use in fire-making without good firewood to build the actual fire. Some-day you may go camping away from home. You should therefore know something about the availability of firewood on various campgrounds.

Today, the choice of firewood is becoming more and more limited on most campsites, and a camper usually has to use what can be found lying around. Of course, on organized sites such as those in national and state parks, firewood, cut in lengths, is kept near the fireplace. Elsewhere, campers must look around for fallen branches and logs of oak, beech, ash, elm, sugar maple, pine, chestnut, poplar, and basswood. These hardwoods have greater fuel value than willow, cedar,

hemlock, tamarack, green pines, and spruce. The latter burn
well enough, but most evergreens throw sparks, which can
prove dangerous on some sites.

The split sections of a log will burn much faster than
unsplit logs. Rotten, crumbly wood is useless, either for kindling or firewood.

MAKING A FIRE BASE   A fire of any sort, whether a campfire or cook fire, has to be built. The degree of skill used in
making a fire foundation is what makes a fire burn.

One good way to make a fire base is to lay three dry sticks
about a foot long on bare ground in the form of an open
"A," as shown in the drawing. (If the ground is wet, a novice
may build a fire on a sheet of aluminum foil.) The top of the

STEPS IN BUILDING A FIRE BASE

"A" must point away from the wind. Put a fair amount of
tinder inside the frame. Place a few pieces of dry kindling,
waiting beside the fire base, on the framework. To protect the
fire, kneel before the fire base with your back to the wind.
Light a match and apply it to the tinder at its lowest point
(the foot of the "A"), since flames travel upward. The little
fire should start right away. When it has taken hold well, dry
kindling can be carefully placed on the fire. Add heavier
kindling and firewood. This fire base can form the foundation
of any fire.

The standard campfires which follow may be built with shorter or longer logs, depending on the size of the fire desired and the space available.

LOG CABIN FIRE   This fire is a popular one. If the fire is for a regular campfire circle, the two base logs can be three feet long, with a diameter of six to ten inches. When the fire circle of about six feet in diameter has been cleared, the two

LOG CABIN FIRE

base logs are laid on it about two and a half feet apart. The next pair of logs should be a little shorter and thinner. Smaller logs are then laid crisscross, as in the drawing, until three or four tiers complete the frame.

Build a heart of tinder and kindling into the fire, once the two lowest tiers are in position. Arrange heavier, dry sticks of varying thickness in tepee form around it, ready to flare up and set the heavier logs afire when the fire is blazing. Boys who are new at fire-lighting may put several crumpled balls of newspaper in with the natural tinder, to assure a quick blaze. They will not show outside the fire frame. Carefully feed sticks, small blocks of wood, and finally small, dry logs into the fire through the top of the framework, as more fuel is needed.

TEPEE FIRE This fire is used chiefly as a fire to start other fires. It is frequently built inside a log cabin fire or crisscross fire (described below under "Cook Fires"). It will not hold its shape, unless built and fed carefully. It is easy to knock over when adding fuel.

TEPEE FIRE

Drive a forked stick into the ground to form the center support of this fire. After the tinder and small kindling have been arranged around this stick, place the larger kindling around it in tepee formation, as illustrated.

"v" FIRE This type of fire is also suitable for campfires. The frame consists of only two hardwood logs from three to five feet in length and six to twelve inches in diameter. Lay the base of the fire all the way along between these two logs.

"V" FIRE

Place thicker sticks on top of the base, so the fire burns between the two logs, as illustrated. This fire can be built up, once there is a good fire burning between the two logs.

Cook Fires

These days, much of the cooking in camps is done on portable stoves of various kinds. In most national and state forests and parks, there are built-in camp grates which must be used for actual fires. Such grates are also installed in nearly all public and private campsites. On some unorganized and out-of-the-way campsites, campers build their own fireplaces or fires. Despite the convenience of stoves, many campers use only wood fires for cooking. Here are some of the many which are effective and simple to build.

DITCH FIRE This primitive fireplace was used by the American Indians of the Plains, who dreaded prairie fires. It is made by digging a ditch long enough and wide enough to take care of the number of pots and the widths of the bottoms of the pots which will be placed over it. This ditch can be about three feet long and from four to eight inches deep. Its width should increase from a few inches at one end to about sixteen inches at the other, so the pots and pans of

DITCH FIRE

various sizes can be set astride the fire. Push the burning wood and embers under the pots as needed. Today, a metal grill placed across this fire trench is a handy way to accommodate pots of various sizes.

HUNTER-TRAPPER FIRE   This fire is usually made by placing two logs, each three feet long and five to eight inches in diameter, about eight to ten inches apart, so the wind circulates between them. The fire is built between the two logs. A stick about three inches thick can be placed under one log about six inches from the end, so more air reaches the fire.

CRISSCROSS FIRE   This fire, which can be built in almost any size, is a fine cook fire. It looks like a log cabin fire

HUNTER-TRAPPER FIRE

foundation. The crisscross fire is a series of tiers of thick sticks and small logs, set side by side as illustrated. It blazes quickly into a bed of red embers and coals which are excellent for roasting potatoes and broiling steaks.

CRISSCROSS FIRE

Cook Stoves

Today, campers everywhere are turning more and more to small portable stoves, rather than fires, to do their cooking. The demands of conservation and stricter fire regulations rule out building fires at many campsites, even in national forests and wilderness areas. With things as they are, cooking in a backyard camp is not much different from camp cooking in wide open spaces.

Camp cook stoves generally burn white gas, butane gas, gasoline, or solid fuel such as charcoal. They usually have from one to three burners. Many of these stoves are so small and light that they can be carried in a pack. Those which weigh less than one and a half pounds can even be carried in a camper's pocket. Despite their small size, they cook efficiently.

CAUTION: The greatest care must be used if one must cook inside a tent. Charcoal stoves can asphyxiate, and many tents are not fireproof.

Cooking Utensils

Few cooking pots and pans are required in a backyard camp, or any camp, for that matter. However, no matter how few cooking utensils a good camper uses, they must be the right sort. Let's see what is really needed in the way of cooking gear.

The first aim is to assemble a cook outfit of minimum weight which will do the best cooking job. The best pots for soups, stews, and the like have wide bottoms which heat their contents quickly and cook fast. Enamel utensils are of little use in camp, because they chip easily and are needlessly heavy. In any camp, pot lids without knobs are best. Lifting rings which fold flat onto the lid should be used instead. Use pots which fit inside each other, if possible.

It is easy to cook nourishing, tasty camp meals. They do not take long to fix, whether the cooking is done on a little camp stove or over a small cook fire.

Cooking meat and vegetables together is a good idea, since it requires only one pot. When making stews, cut the meat and vegetables into small cubes or thin slices for quicker cooking. It takes time to cook on small outdoor stoves, but if you persevere, you will develop the patience of a real cook.

FRYING VS. BROILING   Frying any sort of food in grease, and in a barely hot frying pan at the start, is hard on the digestion. Instead, food such as meat and potatoes should be pan-broiled. This method uses the frying pan, but it should be only lightly smeared with fat or margarine. Make sure the pan is sizzling hot before the meat and vegetables are put into it.

Broiled sardines is a simple dish to make. Just empty a can of sardines, oil and all, into a hot frying pan and broil these little fish about a minute on each side. Do not add oil. Serve on toast.

BOILING   Boiling is an easy, healthful way to prepare most meats, eggs, vegetables, and dried or evaporated fruits, like apples, peaches, apricots, or prunes. Some foods such as meat, potatoes, and turnips, take a long time to cook thoroughly this way. However, provided you put enough water in the pot, you can leave the food to cook without standing over it.

Soups

Nourishing soups will not take the place of meat, eggs, and vegetables in camp, even though there are very fine soups of many varieties on the market today. In a backyard camp, where stores are often nearby, a boy may use some of the fine canned soups available. Directions for preparing each soup are printed on the label, but the ingenious camp cook should experiment with these soups. Many interesting, tasty mixtures may be made by mixing two cans, plus the milk or water called for in the directions. Two cans combined will make five or six good servings. Here are a few suggested soup mixtures:

Vegetable and tomato   Green pea and cream of mushroom
Beef bouillon and tomato   Cream of mushroom and tomato

Dehydrated soups are very good, handy, and lightweight, too. Most of them are mixed with milk or water, and all have cooking directions on the envelopes.

Though evaporated milk may be used in a backyard camp when stores are nearby, powdered milk is nearly as good for making all soups, and much lighter if you have to carry it any distance.

Foil Cookery

Cooking in heavy aluminum foil is an easy way to make simple camp fare a treat. Food in foil may be cooked on live embers and coals, red ashes, or charcoal. Simply wrap the food in foil and twist the ends. A spatula and tongs or a spoon can be used to turn the foil-wrapped food, when necessary, so that it is cooked on both sides.

FOIL-BROILED KABOBS   Nearly all kinds of meat and chicken may be cooked in foil, especially when the meat is cut into 1-inch or 1½-inch cubes. To make foil-broiled kabobs, place part of an onion section between every two meat cubes, and add some tomato cubes, if desired. Season and wrap in heavy foil. Then cook in embers or charcoal about twenty minutes.

HAMBURGERS IN FOIL   Form two hamburger patties of the size you want and season them to taste. Place a slice of raw onion on each hamburger and wrap them both in foil side by side. Set them on red coals or charcoal. They will cook medium-rare in about ten minutes. Turn them over about five minutes after you put them on the coals, so they will be evenly cooked.

FRANKFURTERS IN FOIL   From two to four frankfurters may be wrapped in foil, either individually or in one or two packages. They will cook nicely in about ten minutes. Turn the packages after five minutes, so the franks are cooked evenly on both sides.

FOIL FISH BROIL   Clean, wash, season, and coat small fish with butter. Then wrap in foil and broil about ten minutes, five minutes on each side.

FOIL-COOKED CORN ON THE COB   Remove the silk and outer husks from the ears of corn and let them soak in cold water for half an hour. Then pull the inner husks back and butter the corn, but do not salt it. Draw the inner husks back over the ears. Then wrap them in heavy foil. Do not wrap more than two or three ears together. Cook each package of corn in hot embers or on a charcoal grill, turning the package several times so the ears cook evenly. Single ears should be ready in five or six minutes, but packets of two or three require an additional six minutes. Salt and season the corn only when it is ready to eat.

FOIL BANANA BAKE   This nourishing fruit can be baked

with or without its skin. Try it both ways and see which you prefer. Wrap the banana in foil and cook for three or four minutes. Turn it once while it is baking.

FOIL-BAKED APPLE   Wash an apple and cut it into thin slices. Sprinkle the slices with brown or white sugar, wrap in foil, and bake for three to five minutes. Turn the package over once while it is baking.

Dehydrated Foods

In this space age, experienced campers save time by making simple meals employing dehydrated foods partially or completely prepared in advance. One of the advantages of such foods is their light weight. Even if they must be carried some distance to camp, the rations for a whole day will not average more than one and a half pounds per camper, and varied and satisfactory meals are assured.

Some of the best dehydrated foods are freeze-dry. These foods come in nearly twenty varieties, all of them tasty, excellent, and easily prepared. They take up little room in a pack, which is a big advantage on any camping trip. Freeze-dry foods do not spoil and require no refrigeration.

Various dried, strip meats and mixtures of chipped beef and cheese are also available for camp meals. Many vegetables and salads consisting of raw vegetables in gelatin come in dehydrated form. They are easy to prepare from the directions on each package. These add nourishment and zest to camp food.

4. BEING

OUTDOORS
with
indoor comfort

TO SOME boys, camping out means "roughing it." Every adventurous camper is eager to meet the challenge of outdoor living. Meeting this challenge, however, does not imply that you should not try to make yourself as comfortable as possible.

The American pioneers did not "rough it" in order to prove their hardihood. They were concerned with survival. Consequently, they constantly strove to adapt what little equipment they had to the task of wresting as much comfort as they could from the wilderness. In short, they exercised what has come to be known as good, old-fashioned American ingenuity. You, too, can develop your ingenuity by devising ever more comfortable ways to live in your backyard camp.

Camp Bedding

Blankets, pillows, mattresses, sleeping bags, etc. are an important part of outdoor sleeping comfort.

BLANKETS Wool or part wool blankets are the warmest. With an air mattress or foam pad for insulation a camper usually needs only one good wool blanket for sleeping in the summer. Never choose cotton blankets. They give little warmth and absorb dampness. Dark blankets are best. An old down quilt helps a lot, when a camper has no sleeping bag.

PILLOWS Even hardened cowboys used their saddles as pillows when bivouacking on the range. It is wise to use a small foam rubber or down pillow, or at least a small cushion. An inflatable rubber pillow is often hard. Filling a pillowcase with dry grass or leaves often makes a satisfactory pillow substitute.

MATTRESSES Always have as much bedding under you as

above you. Today, lightweight, waterproof paper mattresses are on the market. They are useful to provide insulation. Paper mattresses are inexpensive and will wear well for a week or so.

The best air mattresses are comfortable, durable, and lightweight. Those used for backpacking trips weigh under three pounds. Rubberized nylon air mattresses are by far the best. With care, they will outlast plastic ones many times over. For real sleeping comfort, tall boys should choose a full-length mattress rather than the "shortie" one, which is only four feet long.

A handy air mattress pump weighs only about half a pound. Fill the mattress until a fist pressed into it will just touch the ground. Then close the valve.

Boys often prefer foam pads, also known as trail beds, to air mattresses. These pads are made of sturdy foam rubber and have a removable, waterproof nylon cover. A foam pad weighs practically the same as an air mattress but provides more insulation and is usually more comfortable.

BLANKET-BEDS A boy should know how to make a blanket-bed so that his covers will stay put through the night. The Klondike blanket roll is a good method of folding two blankets into a comfortable bed roll which stays made. Some

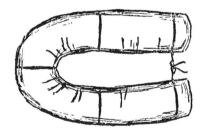

KLONDIKE BLANKET ROLL

gold miners made their blanket-beds in this way during the Klondike gold rush. Sometimes they rolled the bed into a tight bundle, with their few articles of personal gear rolled up inside, and tied it securely in place with a length of rope. At other times, they made it into a long roll, with their personal gear rolled up inside, and tied the ends together with a clove hitch (see Chapter 5). Then they put their heads through these collars and wore them over one shoulder.

Here is one way to make this bed: Lay out a ground cloth on the ground and spread one blanket on it. Then double your other blanket, place it on the first blanket, and tuck it under a few inches at the foot, as shown in step 1. Finally,

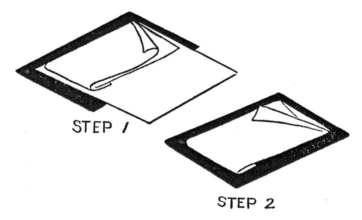

STEP 1

STEP 2

STEPS IN MAKING THE KLONDIKE BLANKET BED

bring the other half of the first blanket over, and tuck it under at the foot also, as in step 2. A few big safety pins, especially made for pinning blankets, will hold them together.

Another blanket-bed is the one-blanket bed. Fold the blanket so it overlaps on one side, as illustrated, and pin it along the side with very large safety pins. Then fold it over a

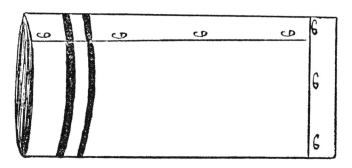

THE ONE-BLANKET BED

few inches at the foot and pin it there also, as shown. Always use a ground cloth even if the ground is dry.

SHEET SLEEPING SACK This easy-to-make sleeping sack keeps your blankets or sleeping bag clean. It is the kind used in the American Youth Hostels. You can make it from five yards of unbleached muslin or from old sheets. The overall length is 78 inches and the width 30 inches when it is completed. There is a 24-inch flap at the top to protect the blanket, and an 18-inch pocket on the underside, at the head,

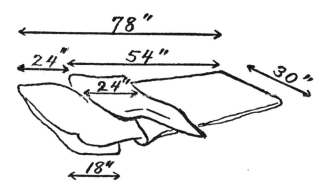

SHEET SLEEPING SACK

to hold a pillow. A gusset on each side gives the sleeper extra room so the sack will not tear. The dimensions are given in the diagram.

SLEEPING BAGS   Instead of using blankets, a boy might choose to use a sleeping bag as his bedding.

Sleeping bags are so handy for sleeping comfortably outdoors, they have almost replaced other bedding. Be careful where you put them, however. No sleeping bag or bedding can be comfortable unless the ground under it is flat and perfectly smooth.

Even inexpensive sleeping bags are comparatively light-weight and serviceable today. By ruling out such expensive materials as eiderdown or goosedown fillers and coverings of the newest synthetic fabrics, one can buy a good, new, serviceable sleeping bag for around ten dollars. It should be light enough to carry easily, not over three pounds.

Never buy a cotton-filled sleeping bag. Such bags give little warmth. They are heavy and always feel moist in damp weather. This is also true of kapok-filled sleeping bags. Labels giving the specifications and telling what filler is used in the bag, are attached to all high-quality sleeping bags. Read these labels carefully.

Choose only a sleeping bag which can be opened, by means of a zipper or snap fasteners, down one side and along the foot. These bags can be opened flat, so they can be aired and given sun baths easily. A closed bag, on the other hand, must be turned inside out when it has to be aired or sunned. By the way, in dry, sunny weather, always air any bedding as soon as you get up in the morning. Either throw it over a bush or hang it up on a tree limb or line.

The snaps or any other metal parts of sleeping bags should be rustproof. Brass or chrome-plated brass hardware is very good.

Zippers are also important. Those made of nylon slide well and when you want them to. When a zipper or other slide fastener will not slide easily, lubricate the track with dry soap, graphite, or candle wax—*never* oil.

Never buy a sleeping bag which has a *waterproof* outer shell, either plastic or rubberized. The outer shell must breathe. All sleeping bags should have *water-repellent,* windproof outer shells. Many good bags have rubber-coated bottoms.

Some sleeping bags have a waterproof canopy which fits above the head. This is not particularly useful. Since good sleeping bags are not waterproof, a camper cannot sleep dry outdoors in wet weather unless he rigs a waterproof fly above the entire sleeping bag.

It is often convenient to stuff a sleeping bag or sleeping gear into a stuff bag. This reduces bulk and protects the sleeping gear.

HAMMOCKS   A jungle hammock is convenient, provided you have two trees, with the right distance between them, to sling it to. The modern hammocks are completely covered with a canopy and are screened to keep out mosquitoes and other bugs. Such hammocks can take the place of a tent and sleeping bag.

CAUTION: Poorly balanced hammocks have a nasty trick of throwing campers out, so it is wise to practice before counting on one as a portable home.

Camp Lighting

There are many ways of lighting a campsite and you can experiment with all of them in your backyard camp. Some campers like lighting which gives a floodlight effect. Others feel that a good camp lantern provides all the light that is necessary. Candle lamps also give a soft light, sufficient for tent lights and most after-dark activities.

Safety should be the prime consideration in choosing camp lighting. Many bad campsite fires have been caused by faulty lighting equipment.

LANTERNS Buy lanterns which burn safe fuel. They should have square, flat bottoms, so that they neither tip over nor roll easily. Lanterns with unbreakable globes are recommended. Today, the very best camp lanterns are resistant to storm, wind, rain, and insects. Pyrex globes are another distinguishing feature of the highest-quality lanterns.

Lanterns which operate on batteries are safe and effective. A number of these excellent lights, powered by flashlight batteries of various sizes, can be bought in some hardware stores and from camp outfitters. Some modern lanterns also burn fuel in disposable cartridges.

Gasoline lanterns are becoming more popular, as modern manufacture makes them safer. Some of them cannot be refilled while lighted and will not spill their fuel even when tipped or overturned. The best of these lanterns have single or double burners. They burn leaded or unleaded gasoline, two pints of which will burn approximately eight to ten hours. They are stormproof, and give a bright, white light. Extra mantles should be carried when such lanterns are used.

Carbide-burning lamps and lanterns are often preferred by experienced campers. Carbide gives a clean, bright light, and a small amount burns a long time.

Kerosene lanterns are not popular, chiefly because of the odor of the fuel. Even a little kerosene accidentally spilled on camp supplies, especially food, will ruin them.

Candle lanterns are a very useful lightweight addition to

camp equipment. The candles should be the short, fat type. Stearic acid candles with a high melting point are best. They do not melt in the heat of summer. Aluminum or other metal frames with mica windows make candles safe to use inside tents.

FLASHLIGHTS   A number of really fine camp flashlights, which stand on a log or hang from a tree branch, are on the market today. Pick a lightweight, two-battery flashlight which throws a good beam of light. A flat shape is preferable. It prevents the light from rolling when it is laid on a log or plank. All flashlight batteries should be packed separately, or reversed, if carried in the flashlight, to prevent contact. Spare batteries and bulbs are musts, as they are for all forms of electric camp lighting equipment.

Mess Kit

With a good lightweight mess kit, a backyard camper can eat in style. The "silverware" should consist of a small stainless steel table knife or a sharp pocketknife, a stainless steel fork, and one large and two small spoons. The kit should also contain a lightweight plate, a deep saucer or small bowl, and a large mug, all of good strong plastic. A small can opener and a bottle opener complete the kit.

Some boys prefer paper plates. Some of these are coated so they can be cleaned with a damp cloth and used several times. After adding a few paper napkins, roll your mess kit in a strong piece of cloth or plastic and tie it with a cord.

Water and Food Storage

Assuring yourself a dependable supply of pure food and water is no problem in a backyard camp. You can go in the house and turn on the tap whenever you want a drink or raid the refrigerator when you feel like having a snack. There's not much fun in doing that, however. You might just as well try to make your backyard camp self-sufficient in food and water for at least a few days. Then if you camp in the woods, you will be fully prepared. Also, a knowledge of how to conserve vital supplies might come in handy in many emergencies, even in your own house.

CANTEENS   To assure pure drinking water on the trail, a canteen is a must. It may be made of polyethylene or plastic, usually canvas or felt-covered. A screw-on cap with a chain is better than a cork.

LISTER BAGS   At a camp in the woods, water is seldom so close that one can get along with a pailful at a time, as needed. Campers who travel far from home usually take along some collapsible bags of canvas or other fabric to store water for cooking and drinking. Lister bags, holding up to thirty gallons or more of water, are a good choice for a small group of campers. These bags are equipped with spigots, and may be hung from a stout branch or stand.

Other water containers are made of close-weave fabrics which permit a loss of about 25 per cent of their contents. They keep the remainder of the water cool by evaporation. Such bags hold from three and a half gallons up and weigh only about a pound. There are also useful plastic jugs and other lightweight, inexpensive plastic water containers. They come in various sizes and handy shapes.

Naturally, the water in these containers will be no cleaner than the water poured into them. If you cannot fill them directly from a spigot, make sure the pail or can you are using is clean. All water which is not known to be safe for drinking or cooking must be purified. This can be done by boiling it hard for ten minutes. Another method is to add chlorine or Halazone tablets to the water, according to directions on the package.

IMPROVISED FOOD COOLERS   There are many ways to keep perishable food without refrigeration. The best methods are discussed here.

Food can be cooled under water. In this method, the food should be in cans or waterproof containers. If screw-top jars are used, be sure the tops are really watertight. Just put the food containers in a tub filled with water and standing in the shade. The same method can be used in a wilderness camp, if a stream is nearby. In this case, be sure to take precautions so that the stream does not wash the food away. Put the containers into an open crate or wooden box and weight it down with stones or rocks. If you wish, you can anchor the crate to a stake on the bank instead.

Food can also be cooled by evaporation. For example, place a food container on four stones above water. Then drape a large piece of burlap or other absorbent cloth over it so that the ends hang down into the water.

Another evaporation cooler can be made by hanging a small, fly-screened crate or cupboard, made of slats, from a handy tree branch near the camp kitchen. Place a basin of water on top of the crate, or hang a pail of water directly above it. Cover the basin or pail with a large piece of absorbent cloth or sacking. Then place a heavy stone in the center of the covering. Allow it to sink to the foot of the basin or pail. Hang the loose ends of the cloth over the food container beneath.

Campers often use a pit cooler to keep food fresh. Before you try this in your backyard camp, however, be sure you have your parents' permission to dig a pit. Even on some organized public and private campsites, pit-digging is not allowed.

In this method, the food is cooled underground. Dig a hole about two or three feet square and about three feet deep, in the shade and conveniently placed. If the earth is crumbly, reinforce the sides with slats or flat pieces of wood. To make this pit really cool—twenty degrees cooler than the outside air—fill it one-third full with gravel or small stones. Pour cold water on the gravel every six or eight hours. Put the food in containers, cans, or a large wood box, into the storage pit. Cover the top of the pit with sticks or branches. Cover the sticks with wet newspapers or cloth for insulation. This type of cooler takes some time to make. However, it is worth it when there are several boys at a camp away from home for a stay of several days or longer.

PROTECTING FOOD FROM ANIMALS AND INSECTS Your food storage cupboard should be well screened against all insects, especially bluebottles and houseflies, which contaminate food.

A backyard camp will probably have fewer animal prowlers than a backwoods camp, but whether one's dinner is eaten by a raiding cat or a raccoon is equally annoying. Put all food which is not in cans in a sack or bucket and suspend it, as illustrated, from a tree or building. The sack should hang about seven feet above the ground.

There are two ways to hang such a food sack. The first method will hold the bundle more securely, but is somewhat complicated. The second method is easier.

In the first method, hold the mouth of the sack tightly closed with a clove hitch. Use the two ends of the hitch to tie a square knot on top of it. For even greater security, tie the ends together again with a square knot, allowing enough slack in the rope to form a small loop. Pass one end of a long rope through this loop. Then tie a bowline on the end of the long rope. Throw the other end of this rope over a tree branch. Pull on the rope to hoist the food bag into the air. Now make the end of the rope fast to the tree trunk or lower branch by means of a clove hitch or two half hitches.

FOOD SACK SUSPENDED FROM TREE

In the second method, simply use one end of the long rope to tie the clove hitch around the mouth of the sack. Then throw the other end of the rope over the branch, hoist the sack into the air, and tie the other end of the rope around the tree trunk or a lower branch with a clove hitch. (For instructions on tying the knots used here, see Chapter 5.)

Of course, sanitation presents no difficulties to backyard campers. On an organized campground, whether a national park or other public campsite, there are toilet and garbage disposal facilities. However, boys should know how to safeguard their health by providing their own sanitation, in case they ever camp on an unorganized site with no facilities.

TOILET KIT   Camp sanitation begins with personal hygiene. Boys who camp away from home should take a toilet kit with them. This should contain a medium-sized cake of good soap, a washcloth, two small absorbent towels, a toothbrush, and tooth paste or powder, a small nail brush, a nail file, and some toilet paper. Roll this kit up in light plastic or carry it in a plastic bag.

GARBAGE DISPOSAL   As much garbage as possible should be completely burned. Empty food cans should be burned, too, then hammered flat and buried at least four feet below ground. An improvised incinerator, made from an old metal container or pail with holes punched around the foot, is handy for burning old paper, cloth, cartons, and the like. If it is permitted to dig holes on an unorganized campsite, a garbage pit about two or three feet square and at least three feet deep should be dug at least 100 feet away from the water supply and tentsite. Some earth or sand should be shoveled on top of each new layer of garbage thrown into the hole.

When breaking camp, this pit should be completely filled in and the earth stamped down into it. Any sod patches removed when digging the pit should be carefully replaced.

DISHWATER DISPOSAL   Dishwater should be poured into a pit, such as the one illustrated. The foot of the pit is covered

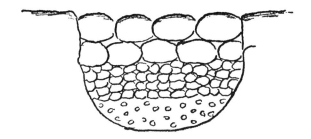

DISHWATER DISPOSAL PIT

with loose sand or gravel topped with a layer of pebbles. Remember, all food scraps should be burned. Only dishwater should be poured into the pit.

LATRINE   Latrines should be made carefully, in order to avoid polluting streams, rivers, and lakes near the campsite. Any latrine should be built below the level of the tentsite, downhill if possible. It should be at least 125 feet away from the water supply.

If possible, make the latrine in an area screened by bushes or trees. When natural cover is lacking, screen it with a tarp or sackcloth supported by poles.

The simplest latrine for a small group of campers is a ditch about three feet long, three feet deep, and sixteen inches wide. Scoop the loose earth from this trench into a pile, running the length of the ditch, at the rear.

Spread soil into the trench each time the latrine is used. Then sprinkle some chlorinated lime on top of the earth in the ditch.

Chlorinated lime is not only a fine disinfectant for the latrine, but also a good fly chaser. This makes it equally valuable for use on the garbage pit, dishwater pit, and the like.

If no chlorinated lime or other disinfectant is available, you can use fire instead. Light a wood fire all along the top of the earth in the trench every second day. Allow it to burn for at least five minutes.

When desired, a simple seat may be made from four strong, straight poles, each about 2½ feet long, lashed in the form of a square. Lash the ends of these poles securely to four strong poles driven deeply into the ground, so that the square straddles the center of the trench.

Hang a roll of toilet paper on one of the upright poles or suspend it from a convenient branch. Put the paper into a strong plastic bag, fastened at the neck with a rubber band, or into a large covered can, to protect it from damp or rain. You may also stick a roll of paper on an upward sloping branch of a convenient bush and cover it with a tin can. Make sure the can has no jagged edges. This method is not always waterproof, however.

A lone camper or two rarely dig a latrine for a one-day or an overnight camp. Instead, each merely digs a small "cat hole" for himself, as needed. It should be about eight inches deep and filled in immediately after use.

STRIKING CAMP   An experienced backyard camper should have little trouble in cleaning up any public or private campsite when he breaks up camp. Nevertheless, he should tackle this job as carefully as any other.

Striking camp is quite as important an operation as setting up camp. A poorly done job may bar a camper from using the site another time. No campground, whether federal, state, or private, wants to have sloppy campers around.

When striking camp, almost as much time should be allowed as for setting it up, especially on an unorganized campsite. However, when chores are taken care of daily, less time is needed.

If a group of boys is camping together, one or two should be assigned to each chore. The latrine, garbage pit, and dish-water disposal pit should really be filled in. The earth should be stamped down, and any turf removed when digging them replaced. The fireplace should be swept clean and returned to its original appearance. All waste paper and remaining trash should be burned carefully or buried. The entire campsite should be left completely clean and looking as it did when the campers arrived.

5.   MASTERING

BASIC
camping
skills

IT IS best to avoid learning things the hard way. There is no point in trying to learn any craft in difficult circumstances or under pressure. That is why a backyard camp is a fine place to learn basic and advanced camping skills.

A boy who knows the fundamentals of knotcraft, direction-finding, and first aid is prepared for many of the most common outdoor emergencies. When a boy has learned these fundamentals by conscientious practice in the relaxed atmosphere of a backyard camp, he will be more likely to keep his head when performing such vital tasks under more difficult conditions.

A knowledge of knot-tying is very useful to campers, hikers, and outdoorsmen in general. You should be able to tie knots and hitches and lash poles together even in the dark or in an awkward position. Knots cannot always be tied when you are sitting in a chair or standing comfortably. If your tent blows down at night, you may have to tie knots in the dark.

You can learn in a very short time to tie the knots, hitches, and lashings in these pages. Just follow the simple pointers given here and look closely at the easy-to-follow drawings. All of these knots will prove very useful in a backyard camp and many other places. A little patience while learning and a lot of practice will enable you to tie each knot correctly and fast. Practice tying knots even with your eyes closed or when blindfolded. Try tying some knots with one hand. Such practice is useful when competing in the contest mentioned in Chapter 9.

Knot-tying Terms

Before learning to tie any knot, you should know the four basic knot-tying terms listed here and study their illustration.

- The standing part is the inactive part of the cord or rope which is worked *on,* but usually not *with.*
- The end can be either end of the rope. In the following instructions and diagrams, the end of the rope that is worked *with* is called "A."
- A loop is made by passing the end of the rope either over or under the standing part. The drawing shows an overhand loop. In an underhand loop, the end of the rope goes under the standing part.
- A bight is made by doubling the rope. It is the curved part of the rope between the end and the standing part.

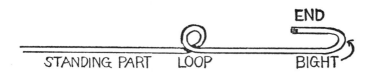

STANDING PART　LOOP　BIGHT　END

KNOT-TYING TERMS ILLUSTRATED

Handy Knots

Most of the knots described below are the ones a backyard camper usually will have need to tie. A couple of ornamental knots are also included.

SQUARE KNOT   This knot, also called the reef knot, has many uses. It is good for tying bandages, because it lies flat and is easy to untie. It is also used for joining the ends of two ropes, tying parcels, and as a knot to tie on top of a clove hitch, using the two ends of the rope which tied the hitch.

To tie: Cross end A over B, toward you, under, then away from you. Then bring end B over A, away from you, under, and toward you. Pull it taut.

THIEF KNOT   This knot looks so much like a square knot, if the ends are covered, that it is impossible to tell them apart. It is a trick knot which sailors used to see if anyone had been rummaging through their ditty bags. A thief in a hurry would not notice that a bag was tied with a thief knot, not a square knot.

To tie: Make a bight in end B and weave end A up through the bight, around B's end and standing part, then back down through the bight, as illustrated. Pull taut. Note in the drawing that the ends are on opposite sides in this knot, whereas they are both on the same side in the square knot.

SHEET BEND   This is a good knot to tie together two ropes of unequal thickness, as well as ropes of the same size.

To tie: First, make a square knot. Then pass end A under its standing part and over the bight of rope B. Pull taut.

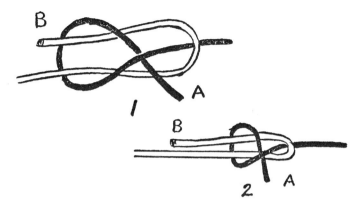

STEPS IN TYING THE SHEET BEND

HALF HITCH   This is a very easy knot to tie. It is useful to use with other knots, and sometimes other knots are built on it. It can be used alone and will not come undone if you tie the end down with string, as illustrated in step 2.

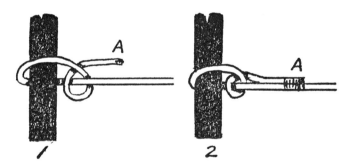

STEPS IN TYING THE HALF HITCH

To tie: Pass end A around a post or through a ring and loop it around its standing part. Then pull the end through the bight. Pull taut.

TWO HALF HITCHES   This knot is the same as the one above, except that it has an extra loop. Two half hitches are useful for fastening the ends of ropes to trees, posts, and mooring rings. Tie the end down with string.

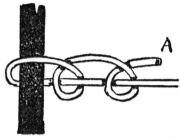

TWO HALF HITCHES

SHEEPSHANK   This knot is used to shorten rope. You should never cut rope to shorten it.

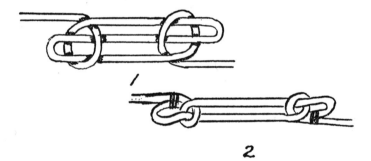

STEPS IN TYING THE SHEEPSHANK

To tie: Make a double bight in the center of the rope. Then tie a half hitch at each end. Tie it with cord as illustrated.

BOWLINE   This knot is used for hitching, hoisting, hauling, and tying around objects. It has many other uses.

BOWLINE

To tie: Use only one end of the rope and leave enough loose end to go around the object, such as your waist, for instance. First make an overhand loop. Then bring the end up through it, around the standing part, and down through the loop again. Pull taut.

CLOVE HITCH
LEFT: HITCH READY TO BE DROPPED OVER TOP OF POST. CENTER: HITCH BEING TIED AROUND POST. RIGHT: HITCH PULLED TAUT AROUND POST.

CLOVE HITCH This hitch is used to attach a rope to a tree, tent, pole, or rail and to begin and end some lashings. It does not slip easily.

To tie: Make an overhand loop and an underhand loop above it, as illustrated. Then drop them over the top of a post, when possible. Otherwise, to tie this hitch around a post, place the rope around the post with end A on the right. Then bring A down over the standing part, around the post again, and up under its bight. Finally, whether you have tied the hitch around a post or not, pull it taut.

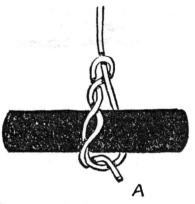

TIMBER HITCH

TIMBER HITCH This knot is useful for dragging poles or logs along the ground or towing them in the water.

To tie: Pass one end of the rope around the pole and bring it over its standing part. Then turn it back on itself three or four times, as illustrated. Pull taut.

ORIENTAL HITCH This simple but effective hitch is used a good deal in Malaya to lash the bamboo walls of huts together and to make tables of bamboo poles.

To tie: Wind the rope around the poles or posts, starting at the center of the rope, as illustrated. Tie the two ends with a square knot around the last post.

ORIENTAL HITCH

PALISADE LASHING The American Indians developed some simple and useful knots. The one given here was used by the Iroquois to lash the poles of their palisades together. It is simple but practical.

To tie: First, tie a clove hitch or two half hitches around the first post, on your right. Then loop the rope around each post, as illustrated, as you work from right to left.

PALISADE LASHING

CAPUCHIN KNOT   This is the decorative knot used by the Capuchin order of monks on their rope belts. It is a fine knot for exhibit and display purposes.

To tie: Make a small bight at one end of the cord or rope. Then make three to six turns around the standing part, as illustrated. Pull both the end and the standing part so the knot will tighten and the bight will merge with the knots.

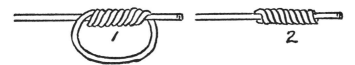

CAPUCHIN KNOT

CHAIN KNOT   This is another good-looking knot used both for decoration and to shorten a rope which is too long.

To tie: Make a small loop so the rope passes over its standing part. Pass a stick or dowel, a few inches long, between the standing part and the loop, to hold the links of the chain in place. Pass end A up through the loop from the left, around, then up through the new loop. Continue until you have made as many loops as you wish, tightening the loops as you progress so they are even in size. At the end, reverse

Mastering Basic Camping Skills—77

the final loop by bringing the end up behind its own standing part, at the right, before passing it down through the loop. Bring end A up through the loop, at the right, around its standing part and down through the final loop. Pull taut.

CHAIN KNOT

Direction-finding

A backyard camp is an ideal place to learn compass- and map-reading. To be sure, a boy camping in his backyard isn't going to get lost! But this is all to the good. A boy can learn everything better when he is relaxed. Reading a map or compass incorrectly while on a trip in the backwoods can have serious consequences. There is no such danger in a backyard camp.

Furthermore, a backyard camp is a very good place to check the accuracy of compasses and to learn how to orient maps correctly. Every boy ought to know what landmarks visible from his house lie due north, east, south, or west. If a compass indicates that a landmark, known to lie in a westerly direction, is towards the north, obviously the compass is faulty. It's better to find this out before leaving home than on the trail.

READING COMPASSES A good compass is a very useful instrument for indicating direction and helping campers find the way to various objectives. It need not be expensive. One of the best inexpensive compasses has a dial needle with a catch to hold it in place and a snap-shut cover. One end of the needle, which is protected by the compass cover, points north and the other end points south.

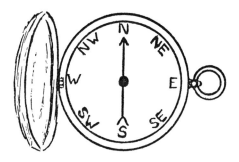

COMPASS

On some compasses, the end of the needle which points north is shaped like an arrow or distinctively colored. If your compass has no such feature, check it against a known direction or the sun. Be certain to remember which end of its needle points north.

Now, learn at least sixteen points of the compass by heart. They may prove very useful one day. The following compass points are all you need to know to find your way or orient a map: N (North), NNE (North-North-East), NE (North-East), ENE (East-North-East), E (East), ESE (East-South-East), SE (South-East), SSE (South-South-East), S (South), SSW (South-South-West), SW (South-West), WSW (West-South West), W (West), WNW (West-North-West), NW (North-West), and NNW (North-North-West). (There is a compass game called "Boxing the Compass" in Chapter 8, which helps boys learn the compass points.)

Though a boy can travel directly north by glancing occasionally at his compass, he might wish to go northward from point to point. This is known as aligning the way or sighting with a compass. It works in any direction toward which a camper wants to travel. Here's how to proceed.

Hold the compass out flat in front of you. Be sure that it is away from all metal. This allows the dial needle to swing freely so that its business end points north. Turn the compass gently, until the "N" on its face is under the end of the needle which points north. The compass is now oriented so that all of the compass points face in the correct directions.

Note a prominent tree, rock, or other landmark which is directly north and hike to it. Once there, pick out another landmark directly north, by reference to your compass, and hike to it. This is the way to travel north by alignment. To travel south, simply walk away from north, in the opposite direction. So long as you know where north is, you will be able to align your way to the east or west by picking out landmarks and going to them.

CAUTION: Never leave or store a compass near metal objects. This destroys its ability to indicate north or any other direction.

ORIENTING MAPS Studying a good, large-scale topographical map in a backyard camp provides a good idea of the lay of the land, stretching out in all directions. North is at the top of most good maps. Orienting a compass so that its needle also points north gives a double check on the position of landmarks and surrounding points suitable for future hikes. Fine, clear maps have a scale of at least one inch to a mile.

Excellent maps may be secured at low cost through the United States Geological Survey, Department of the Interior, Washington, D.C. Many maps of various areas can often be obtained free by writing to big oil companies, automobile clubs, and similar sources.

MAKING TREE BLAZES   Campers in the woods today still use tree blazes as an aid in direction-finding. However, there is a difference between the tree blazes they use and those made by American pioneers in the days when the need for conservation was not so apparent as it is today.

Instead of disfiguring trees with ax or knife scars, modern campers mark trails by "blazes" cut from strong, thick cardboard or plywood, painted or varnished to make them fairly weatherproof. You can cut these blazes from material in pieces about four inches square. The blazes can be round, square, or diamond-shaped. Paint them with bright colors,

TREE BLAZES

such as yellow, orange, or scarlet, for good visibility. Fasten them by a spot of adhesive or a tack to trees on the trail to be followed.

Safeguarding Health

There is almost as much chance of being injured physically when engaged in camp activities in a backyard camp as when camping in a forest or wilderness. Insurance companies know that by far the greatest number of accidents take place in and around the home. So it can be in a backyard camp. That is why a boy should learn to play it safe in his backyard camp. By doing so, he will learn to be more alert, cautious, and careful if he camps farther afield.

Safety is really a combination of quick thinking plus common sense. Boys who feel or have been told that they are accident-prone should be doubly careful. Some boys are careless. Others tempt fate by acting like daredevils. The following incidents illustrate some freakish predicaments which boys have brought upon themselves.

Once a camper got his bare foot stuck under the door of a small outdoor toilet and could not get it out again. Another time, a boy caught his head between the bars of a metal fence. He was demonstrating that if his head could go through an opening, the rest of him could, too. It couldn't! Another boy thrust his thumb into an eighteen-inch length of iron pipe in order to prove that the pipe would come off easily. It didn't!

To be sure, these boys were all rescued from their self-made predicaments, but how much better it would have been if they had never got into such trouble in the first place!

SAFETY POINTERS Following these rules will prevent many accidents common in any type of camp.

- Never use a charcoal stove or kerosene heater to heat a tent or even a lean-to. There is grave danger from deadly escaping carbon monoxide fumes.
- Never run or play in your backyard camp until you have filled in any holes and cleared away loose stones, sticks, firewood, and broken glass. Be sure to remove or raise any low-hanging clothesline or wires to well above adult head-level.
- Never leave garden implements lying around. Campers can injure their feet badly by stepping on the teeth of a rake, carelessly left lying in long grass. And both boys and grownups can get a king-size bang on the head from the handle of a rake by stepping on the teeth of a rake which has been stood up against a tree—for safety!

- Never walk around your backyard camp after dark. Darkness can cause bad falls and collisions.
- Never break branches or sticks across the knee. Sticks should be broken under the foot, by pulling one end upward.
- Never poke fingers or hands into interesting-looking holes in walls, trees, logs, or woodpiles, especially after dark. Do not peek into them, either. Animals or snakes may live there and might bite.
- Never scratch mosquito bites or those of other insects. Infections, many far worse than the bites, may follow.
- Never lift heavy objects without bending your knees.
- Avoid tripping over tent pegs and guy ropes.
- If a tent ever catches fire, down it immediately! The fabric will smother the flames.

This listing stops here in order to give you a chance to take stock of your own backyard camp. Try to think of all the ways in which you could get hurt. Then remove the causes of such possible accidents.

AVOIDING THE POISON IVY MENACE   Fortunately, there are few plant pests to plague campers, whether in a backyard camp or one situated in the wilds. It is hard to avoid poison ivy, however. This obnoxious plant grows in most states.

The accompanying drawing shows what poison ivy looks like. Note its three-fingered leaf grouping. Its leaves are shiny green in spring and summer, changing to a mottled reddish yellow in fall. It is found practically everywhere. This is not surprising, considering that poison ivy roots can grow to well over a mile in length. Poison ivy grows on the ground. It climbs bushes, trees, and posts. It is even found in sheds. The plant outstrips its destruction by man.

POISON IVY

It is hard to kill the roots of poison ivy without blasting every surrounding plant. When it is found growing alone, however, rock salt spread around its stalks should kill it.

It is inadvisable to pull poison ivy up by the roots, even when wearing heavy gloves. Such gloves would have to be washed afterward with very strong soap to prevent them from infecting yourself or others. Burning the plant is also unwise, since the smoke from the fire would infect anyone passing through it.

The best way to avoid the poison ivy menace, therefore, is to label it. Drive a long, round-topped stake, painted bright yellow or red for visibility, into the ground where poison ivy grows in your camp. This will warn you to keep clear of the plant.

If you think poison ivy is not bad enough to make such a fuss about, just ask anybody who has had a run-in with the pesky plant. Treatment for poison ivy infection is given later in this chapter.

AVOIDING INSECT PESTS Many insects will leave a camper alone if he leaves them alone. A camper who gets stung by a yellow jacket, wasp, hornet, or bee often has himself to blame. Don't be foolish enough to chop at a hollow log because you see a yellow jacket fly into it. Don't figure you can knock a hornets' nest off a tree branch and get away before the vengeful insects see you. You can't! Avoid eating bread, covered with jam or honey, outdoors. This attracts bees and wasps.

Other insects, like mosquitoes, no-see-ums, horseflies, and deerflies, do not return the favor of being left alone. A good insect repellent, perhaps in bomb or spray form, will help to scare them off. Deerflies, the fastest flying insects, and horseflies bite hard. However, they hesitate for just a moment, after landing, before they bite. That is the time to swat them.

Treatment for insect bites is discussed under "First Aid" below.

First Aid

A boy should know not only how to avoid common outdoor hurts and accidents, but also how to treat them if and when they occur. Since accidents happen suddenly, a backyard camper should be prepared to render first aid quickly and correctly on the spot at any time. He should buy a good first aid handbook and read about the most common accidents and the best way to treat them. Boys can take turns practicing bandaging, one boy acting as patient while another applies some of the easier bandages.

One of the most important parts of first aid is to be able to keep one's head under difficult conditions. It is also important to think and act fast and correctly. The injured person may be bleeding a great deal. Excited bystanders often give wrong advice. So to be of real service, the first aider must keep calm and do what he knows to be right. Even grownups will listen to a boy who appears to know his business.

Prompt, skillful first aid often saves the lives of injured persons, but remember that first aid means giving help only until a doctor takes over. Too much first aid may prove more harmful to the patient than too little.

Below, listed in alphabetical order, are some of the injuries which you may be called on to treat. The treatments described are not difficult and require only the simplest first aid equipment.

CAUTION: Never treat a patient for any wound unless your hands are very clean.

BLISTERS AND CHAFING Blisters and chafing are usually caused by rubbing or pressure, often inside ill-fitting shoes. Like many other trivial injuries, blisters which are neglected may become seriously infected.

When a blister is just beginning to form, sponge it with an antiseptic solution. Then cover it with a fairly wide piece of adhesive tape. Leave the tape on for a few days, to allow time for new skin to form under the blister.

Gently sponge broken blisters with a medicated soap or antiseptic solution. Pierce any remaining blister near the edge with a sterilized needle and gently squeeze the fluid out. Then cover the blister with a sterile dressing, fastened in place by a gauze bandage or adhesive tape.

BRUISES A bad bruise can cause swelling and pain. It may be helped by applying cold compresses or wrapping the bruise in a towel soaked in cold water.

BURNS Burns and scalds may be slight or serious. Serious burns are a doctor's job. To treat minor burns and scalds, gently smear the injury with a good burn ointment. Then cover the burn with a sterile pad, either bandaged in place or attached with adhesive tape.

The newest relief for burns is to immerse the burned part in cold water. When the affected part cannot be immersed, cold water compresses can be applied instead.

CUTS AND WOUNDS   These frequent camp injuries are often caused by using a knife or ax improperly. (See Chapter 7 for ways to prevent such accidents.)

Cuts and wounds may be dealt with under "Bleeding" or "Hemmorhage" in a first aid book. The bleeding may be slight or profuse. If the bleeding is severe, follow the treatment outlined in your first aid manual. If the bleeding is not severe, bathe the cut quickly with medicated soap and water. Then press a compress firmly on top of the injury to stop the bleeding. Next, put a fresh compress on the wound and bandage it securely with a gauze bandage or adhesive tape.

To avoid infecting the cut, be certain that everything which touches it is perfectly clean. This means clean hands, clean water, a clean compress, and a clean bandage.

FRACTURES   Do not treat any fracture, other than to see that the patient is not moved or allowed to move. Some first aid books advise immobilizing the fractured part. However, the amateur trying to do so is just as likely to turn a simple fracture into a compound one. Treatment of fractures is work for a doctor.

INSECT BITES AND STINGS   Insect bites are seldom serious unless they are scratched. Scratching hard is a natural reaction, but it may cause a nasty infection, far worse than the worst itch. Bathe bites with a strong antiseptic medicated soap. Better still, use a counter-irritant, such as aromatic spirits of ammonia. Slight pain, for just a minute or so, is far better than acute itch. Calamine lotion or a thick paste of baking soda is also helpful when applied to the irritation.

In the case of a sting caused by a wasp, bee, or hornet, remove the stinger from the flesh as quickly as possible with tweezers or the point of a sterilized needle or pin. (A needle can be sterilized by holding it in the flame of a match for a few seconds.) Bathe the puncture with a fairly strong antiseptic solution. Then apply spirits of ammonia or calamine lotion.

POISON IVY INFECTION   Some campers go to doctors for injections which provide immunity to poison ivy. However, these shots are not always effective. A boy who has touched poison ivy with his hands should keep them away from his face and any other part of his body. Above all, never scratch poison ivy itch. This may cause serious infection.

Wash any part of your body which has contacted the plant with green soap or yellow laundry soap. This helps, but it is not a cure.

As soon as possible, sponge the affected parts with soothing calamine lotion. Or dissolve boric acid or Epsom salts in boiling water—a heaping teaspoon to each pint of boiling water.

Applying aromatic spirits of ammonia helps to neutralize the ivy poison. Never use an oily liquid or ointment on poison ivy itch. It will only spread the infection. Some doctors give a prescription, for internal use, as a treatment for poison ivy infection.

SPRAINS   Wrists and ankles are sometimes sprained around camp. The usual sprains are treated by putting cold compresses on them. Soaking the entire hand or foot in a basin of cold water helps. Sometimes using hot water, right after cold, relieves the pain. Gently massaging the sprain with liniment also helps.

FIRST AID KITS   Every backyard camper should have a few first aid articles handy. They should be contained in a small plastic case or rolled in a small square of strong plastic or waterproof fabric.

First aid kits may be bought from most drug stores and sports outfitters, but you can save money by assembling your own. It should contain the following items: band-aids of various sizes; two or three gauze bandages, from one to three inches wide; one or two compresses; adhesive tape; merthiolate swabs; an ointment for burns; sunburn cream; calamine lotion; a small pair of tweezers; a few safety pins; insect repellent; and hydrogen peroxide, 3% volume.

Hydrogen peroxide is among the simplest antiseptic solutions to use in those first aid treatments described above which call for an antiseptic solution.

The above kit is large enough for personal use. However, when you are camping with a few friends or on a camping trip by yourself, you should have a larger kit, such as the one described below.

Bandages and Dressings

Adhesive tape, medicated and waterproof	Sterile gauze pads and dressings, assorted sizes
Adhesive patches and band-aids, assorted sizes	Gauze bandages, 1- and 2-inch widths
Triangular bandages, two	

Instruments

One pair of good scissors	Wooden spatulas
Swabs, sterile, cotton-tipped	Safety pins, assorted sizes

One pair of sharp-pointed tweezers

Needles and thread
Small plastic measure

Medications

Hydrogen peroxide, 3% volume
Aromatic spirits of ammonia
Ointment (for burns)
Baking soda (for burns)
Sunburn lotion
Salt tablets
Chlorine or Halazone tablets (for purifying water)
Boric acid (for eye antiseptic solution)

Tincture of merthiolate
Green or other antiseptic soap
Calamine lotion
Laxative
Excedrin tablets (for headache)
Liniment (for sprains)
Insect repellent

CAUTION: Keep all first aid kits out of reach of small children.

6. MAKING

WHAT
you
need

THERE IS nothing like a backyard camp for encouraging good old-fashioned American ingenuity. By making much of his own equipment, a boy can really stretch his allowance. Besides, he will gain the increased self-confidence that comes with doing things for himself.

Improvising Your Own Shelter

You can improvise your own backyard shelter for a fraction of the cost of a ready-made tent. Practically the entire expense incurred in making such a shelter is the cost of the material, which is bought by the yard.

To make these shelters, a piece of lightweight, weatherproof material is required. A lightweight tarp can be used, but it will cost more and be heavier. It should be twice as long as it is wide. Its dimensions will depend on how big a shelter you want. Usual sizes range from 6 x 12 to 8 x 16 feet. For smaller boys, a 5 x 10 will do. There are three different ways, illustrated below, in which these shelter-tents may be made easily from this same oblong of fabric.

First, practice folding a strong piece of paper measuring 2 x 4 inches as shown in the following diagrams. Then it will be easy to fold the fabric in the same way when setting up your tent.

The point marked "A" on the drawings should be reinforced by a half-circle of strong fabric such as canvas. This will take the strain of supporting the shelter where it is held in place by a short pole or, in the wedge shelter, where the ends are supported by the cord. Such patches are made by cutting a circle of strong cloth 9 to 12 inches in diameter in half. They are sewn to the inside of the shelter fabric at point A (and also at point B in the wedge shelter).

A 12-inch length of strong tape or cord should be doubled

and the center sewn to each corner of the fabric. In this way, the tapes may be fastened to tent pegs. Another way to peg this type of shelter to the ground is to tie the tape around a strong metal ring, sewn or tied with the clove hitch at each corner. Then push a slim metal or wooden tent peg through the ring.

THE WEDGE SHELTER This is the easiest tent to make. Simply double the cloth and hang it over a strong cord or thin rope, suspended between two trees or posts, as illustrated. String the rope about four feet above the ground. If it is strung higher, there will be less room inside the tent. (This also applies to the height of tent poles, so it is well to count four feet as most suitable for both the rope and the poles, which may also be used in the other two models below.)

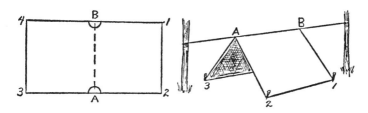

WEDGE SHELTER

A wedge shelter, made from a tarp 6 x 12 feet and slung over a rope four feet from the ground, will be about nine feet wide inside. This is roomy enough for two boys. For a one-boy shelter, a 6 x 10 tarp will suffice. This will reduce the inside width to about six and a half feet.

This shelter can be made into a standard tent by sewing a wedge-shaped piece of fabric at each end. Cut one of the wedges exactly down the center to form the two door flaps.

This door may be tied shut, in case of rain, by sewing 6-inch lengths of strong tape, opposite each other, on both flaps. Two or three sets of ties may be sewn on, as desired. If only two are used, one should be about six inches from the ground and another about halfway to the top. If three are used, they should be about equally spaced. A better but more difficult way to close the tent flaps is to sew on a strong zipper.

THE TRIANGLE SHELTER This shelter can be suspended from a convenient branch by a strong cord attached to point A, preferably with the clove hitch (see Chapter 5). Once pulled really tight, this hitch will hold the fabric securely. The triangle shelter may also be tied by a tape at point A to a cord, stretched about four feet above the ground between two trees, as illustrated for the wedge. When point A has been made fast, peg points 1 and 4 to the ground. Then peg points

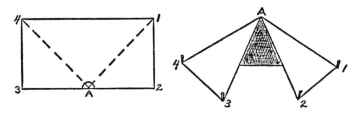

TRIANGLE SHELTER

2 and 3. The folds in this shelter, from point A to points 1 and 4, are illustrated by the broken lines in the diagram.

A center pole, about four feet long, may be used to pitch this shelter. A pole takes up space, however, so the cord suspension method is best.

A door may be sewn onto this model, if desired, in the same way as for the wedge shelter above.

THE SEMIPYRAMID SHELTER This shelter may be suspended in the same way as the triangle model above. Because of the difference in shape, tapes must be sewn on at points 2, 3, 5 and 6. The four folds are shown in the drawing by broken lines. Points 1 and 4 are tucked inside the tent to form

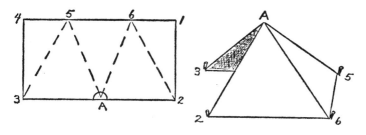

SEMIPYRAMID SHELTER

a partial floor. Their position is decided by the height of the tent peak from the ground and the strain on the shelter when pegged. First, peg points 2 and 3 to the ground. Then peg points 5 and 6. For this model, too, a center pole may be used when there is no other convenient means to suspend it.

It is good practice to make all these shelters, to see which you prefer, especially since the materials required for all three are the same.

Camp Gadgetry

The backyard camper can make a number of gadgets that come in handy in any camp. The lack of wildwood material, such as straight saplings and thin straight branches, is no handicap. Even on organized campsites away from home, the cutting of saplings is contrary to good conservation practice and is often forbidden. Moreover, the dowels, broom handles, and odd poles which have a way of turning up around a backyard camp actually provide better material than can be found on a public or private campsite. It is very difficult to find straight branches and saplings of the right thickness, even in wooded country.

The gadgets described here will make fine displays for the campcraft exhibit discussed in Chapter 9.

FIREWOOD CARRIER   A firewood carrier can easily be made from a piece of canvas or other stout cloth about 15 inches wide and 40 inches long. Double the cloth lengthwise and cut an oval approximately 6 inches long and 3 inches wide from the center of the top, leaving 4½ inches on each side. Overlap these pieces one and a half inches and sew

FIREWOOD CARRIER

them with strong carpet thread. Pass a straight, stout hardwood stick about eighteen inches long and one and a half inches in diameter through and under the two ends, as illustrated. The wood tote is complete. Of course, it can be made smaller or larger.

AX SHEATH   Most good axes, especially those of the belt type, are sold with a sheath. However, if your ax has no sheath, you can easily make one from a strong piece of leather or canvas.

Here is how to draw the sheath pattern of the size necessary to cover your ax neatly. Fold a piece of paper in half. Place the axhead on it, making allowance for the width of the back of the blade. Trace around the ax blade on both sides of the fold in the paper. Allow an extra half-inch along the lower edge and the cutting edge, in order to allow space for the lacing. Then draw the flap, allowing for the width of the ax along the top.

Cut a ⅛-inch strip of heavy leather, the shape of the cutting edge, to sew into the front of the sheath. If you prefer, you can double a half-inch strip of tough leather and sew it in place along the cutting edge. Either type of strip will protect the lacing from the sharp blade of the ax.

Place the pattern onto the leather you are going to use for the sheath. Trace it onto the leather. Punch four small holes through the leather and make a vertical cut to join each two

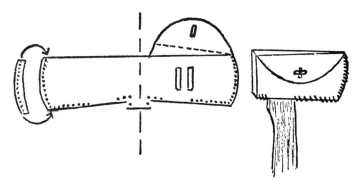

AX SHEATH
LEFT: SHEATH PATTERN. RIGHT: AX IN FASTENED SHEATH.

holes, as illustrated. These openings should be made in the part with the flap—the larger half. A belt can be slipped through these slits, if desired.

Cut a narrow, short slit on the flap, as illustrated, and sew a hardwood toggle or leather knot to the other side, directly under the slit, as a fastening.

The corresponding holes along the underside and cutting edge of the sheath make it easy to lace the sheath together with a leather lace, tough round thong, or strong cord.

POT HOOKS These can be made from tough, forked branches about a foot long. Even better ones can be made by using large "S" hooks which can be bought at most ten-cent stores or hardware stores. They can also be made from pieces of strong, heavy wire. Bend each piece into an "S" shape, as illustrated.

HOMEMADE POT HOOKS

TREE COLLAR This is a handy gadget on which you can hang cooking utensils from "S" hooks. The collar is fastened around a handy tree or a tent pole. Merely force one end of each "S" hook through a small hole made with an awl in a web belt about two inches wide. Make the holes about three inches apart. The kitchen utensils, or a flashlight or lamp, hang down from the other end of each "S" hook, as illustrated.

A more elaborate collar can be made by folding a piece of strong white canvas into a three-inch strip and sewing it so that it remains that way. Just sew galvanized "S" hooks onto

TREE COLLAR

it or force them through holes, as above. Fasten the collar with a buckle or tape ties at the ends, to hold it around a tree or tent pole. This collar can be decorated by painting a design on it.

TOASTING FORKS   A handy fork for toasting frankfurters, marshmallows, etc. over a fire can be made by straightening a coat hanger and bending it into the shape of a fork, as illustrated. Similar forks, with one or two prongs, may be made from thin, short lengths of wood.

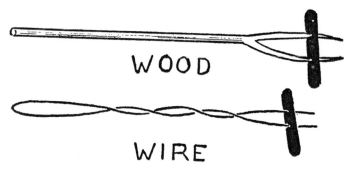

WOOD

WIRE

HOMEMADE TOASTING FORKS

HAND GUARD   This handy gadget may be used on a toasting fork or the handle of a pot or pan. It is easily made from a strong paper plate or, for a more permanent job, a foil plate. Make a hole in the center with an awl. Enlarge it just enough for the handle of the fork or pan to pass through it. You will appreciate this gadget, as it provides protection from the heat of a small, bright blaze.

HAND GUARD

WIRE-AND-FOIL GRIDDLES AND GRILLS   By straightening and rebending wire coat hangers, a backyard camper can make a number of handy cooking utensils. The illustration shows two griddles made from coat hangers and strong foil which has been folded around the wires so it will stay in place.

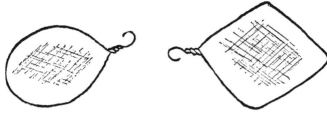

By laying a few lengths of wire across the top of a griddle made from coat-hanger wire, without using foil, a boy can make a regular grill on which meat and other things may be roasted. The ends of the lengths of wire should be bent over with a pair of pliers to hold them in place.

FOIL FRYING PANS A wire-and-foil griddle can be converted into a shallow frying pan by pushing the foil down a little below the wire before pressing the foil into shape. A frying pan can also be improvised from foil alone. Use a piece of heavy foil, or two pieces placed one on top of the other. Form the foil into a small, square frying pan by folding up the edges an inch or two, as required. Then squeeze the ends together at each corner.

Vegetables and meats which do not take long to cook may be cooked in the foil frying pan while you, the chef, look on.

TIN CAN UTENSILS It is not wise to try to make cooking utensils from most tin cans. True, cooking kits made from tin cans look fine in pictures and serve well enough in case of emergency. Nevertheless, many campers have been very badly cut from trying to make such cooking gear. The process requires special shears and pliers—*not* an ax or knife—

plus a knowledge of tincraft. Without these, you had better leave tincraft alone.

This advice, of course, does not apply to well-made shortening cans. They make good water buckets. Also, when the top has been cleanly cut off with a can opener, such a can may be used for baking corn in the husk or potatoes in the embers. However, even these cans may have a sharp or jagged edge which should be flattened before use.

FIRE GRATES Heat-resistant, lightweight metal rods and pipes make very handy fire grates. Three- and four-point grates are easy to make. Simply drive three or four strong metal rods or pieces of pipe, about 12 to 18 inches long and ½-inch to ¾-inch in diameter, into the ground in the form of a triangle or square. Light the fire between the metal rods, and set the pot on top of them.

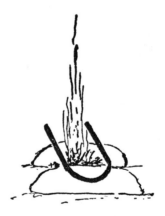

"U" GRATE

The "U" grate is also a very useful cooking grate which can be made in a backyard camp. It is handy enough to take to any camp. Simply bend a 3-foot length of a ½-inch or ¾-

inch metal rod into a "U" shape. Put it on top of two flat-topped stones, about seven inches high. Build the fire between them, directly under the arms of the "U."

WASH BASIN STAND   This simple stand will prove useful in any camp for holding a wash basin. You will need three poles or dowel sticks, about three and a half feet long and about one inch in diameter. Lash them together with a piece of strong twine or cord about a foot from the top. You can use a clove hitch for this (see Chapter 5). Wind the ends around the poles a few times and tie them together with a square knot. Then spread the legs out. Place a wash basin in position, as illustrated, so the basin is about two and a half feet from the ground.

WASH BASIN STAND

WINDBREAK   A windbreak is not only handy in a backyard camp, but also can be used as a protection against wind and blowing sand at the beach or lakeshore. A screen of this sort also provides protection from the elements when set up around the head of a sleeping bag. It may also be used to shelter a portable stove from the wind. These windbreaks are easy to make and may be made in various heights and lengths.

Strips of canvas, duck, or other strong, windproof fabric may be bought in widths ranging from 3 to 3½ feet and in lengths ranging from 10 to 20 feet, depending on the size screen desired. Fold such a strip over about three inches at each end to make a sort of pocket. Sew each pocket with strong carpet thread. Be sure to sew the tops of the pockets also, so that the rods used to support the screen will not come through them. Also sew two pockets one-third of the way from each end, as illustrated.

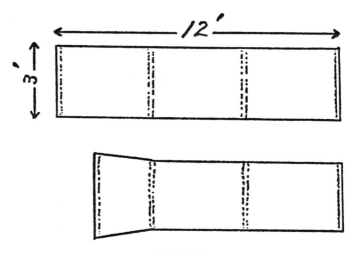

WINDBREAK
BROKEN LINES SHOW POCKETS. **TOP:** DIMENSIONS. **BOTTOM:** AS SET UP IN AN "L" SHAPE.

The windbreak is held in place by 1-inch or 1½-inch hardwood dowel sticks. For driving into soft sand, choose sticks about six feet long. Shorter dowels may be used when the screen is placed on hard earth. If you wish, lightweight metal rods may be used as supports instead.

Windbreaks can be set up in various shapes, such as an "L," "V," crescent, oblong, or square, depending on the number of pockets and dowels used.

Personalizing Your Camp

By using just a little imagination, a boy can add many personal colorful touches to his backyard camp. They will indelibly stamp the camp with his personality and distinguish it from all other camps. Also, they will show the pride a boy takes in his handiwork.

CAMP PENNANTS These little flags come in handy to identify a campsite or tentsite when a number of tents are grouped together. They may be made in various ways. Almost any piece of strong, colored cloth or felt is suitable. Each pennant should be from eight to twelve inches long and three or four inches wide at the broad end.

Double two strips of the material, each about half an inch wide and about a foot long, at the center. Sew these strips on as tie tapes at the broad end. Pennants can be hung from tent ropes or guys. They are also handsome when tacked or tied onto a pole just outside the tent.

These streamers can be just as decorative as the skill of the maker allows. You can paint brightly colored designs on the cloth or decorate it with the name of your camp and/or a personal crest. A small camping group can adorn its pennant with the crest and name of the club.

CAMP SIGNS Backyard camps are as much entitled to a colorful name and crest as a camp deep in the wilderness.

Camp name signs can be about 10 x 16 inches or larger, as decided by the camper or camping group. They may be painted on stout cardboard which has already been painted to make it showerproof, or on cloth glued to cardboard. Of course, fairly permanent signs are best. They may be cut from thin plywood or strong board which does not need to be more than half an inch thick. The designs can be painted directly onto them.

TRAIL SIGNS   These signs may be cut from plywood or board, about 4 x 14 inches or larger, in a rustic style. They are very suitable for any camp. If your backyard camp covers quite a lot of ground, signs such as "Upper Trail" and the like may be made in the same way as the camp name sign.

7. GETTING

THE MOST
out of
your gear

PART OF camping fun lies in getting the most serviceable and longest-lasting equipment at the best possible price. Much of the camp gear used today is better, more practical, and lighter weight than that sold only a few years ago. Much time and money have been spent in experimenting with outdoor equipment, with the result that camp outfitters are now turning out improved gear at reasonable prices.

Real bargains are often to be found in new and used surplus camp equipment. This applies especially to new cooking kits, personal gear, tents, ground cloths, sleeping bags, and air mattresses. Great care must be taken, however, when buying used gear, even when it is apparently in good condition. Sleeping bags and air mattresses, in particular, should be carefully inspected before any deal is closed.

Buying camp equipment is more fun when it is done in a store which has a good selection of gear. If this is not possible, however, a boy can order items by mail from a department store or a reliable mail order house. Such firms will send an illustrated catalog on request. Most of them sell good, modern camp equipment of all sorts at reasonable prices and stand behind the quality of their goods.

CAUTION: Never order any surplus sleeping bags, whether new or used, by mail. Such bags should always be examined thoroughly and chosen personally.

Why Not Rent?

It often pays to rent camp gear rather than buy it. Renting any item provides an opportunity to find out how satisfactory it is. It eliminates the possibility that a backyard camper will be stuck with equipment he doesn't like. If a rented item passes the test, it can be bought later.

A backyard camp is an ideal place for testing all kinds of equipment. If you can't decide what kind of tent to buy, for instance, try renting one first. You will find out soon enough whether the tent is roomy enough. It's also easy to find out whether or not a tent is weatherproof. Just spray a garden hose on it.

Good camp gear, from tents and sleeping bags to cooking utensils, can be rented at reasonable prices in some outfitting stores in larger towns. Otherwise, the gear has to be rented by mail. Some outfitters ask for an advance deposit, to cover possible damage to equipment.

At the end of the camping period, everything must be dried thoroughly, packed carefully, and returned to the place from which it was rented. It takes care to return everything in one lot. Remember that any claims for damage to tents and other gear can add considerably to the original rental cost.

It goes without saying that whether a boy buys or rents his equipment, he should deal only with reputable outfitters.

Camp Clothing

The backyard camp is an ideal place for testing camp clothing and footwear. Serious thought should be given to really durable, comfortable clothing for camping.

Once you know what to choose, you can look around until you find the needed items at a reasonable price. Of course, you may find the camp clothes you need right in your clothes closet. Better look there first!

The old, comfortable clothes worn in a backyard camp are just about the same as experienced campers wear in wilderness campsites. What a camper wears on parents' days in an organized boys' camp is the same as he would wear to welcome visitors to his backyard camp.

Many top camp outfitters and big department stores have camp clothing counselors. Their title makes them sound important. They are, too, but you can learn to be your own clothing counselor by reading this chapter. In no time at all, you will be able to advise your friends what to wear in camp.

MAKING SURE IT FITS　Comfort in clothes means, first of all, the correct fit. This is not too big and certainly not too small. A boy is better off with camp clothing which fits easily, though a little big, than wearing what appears to be the exact size. You will know whether the camp longs you are trying on are too tight. Just touch your toes a few times. The same test will reveal whether a shirt should be a little bigger in the shoulders or longer in the sleeves.

Comfort in clothing must begin at the time of purchase, not after a week or two of discomfort, while it is being broken in. Don't accept the statement of the salesman that trousers or a shirt will fit fine after a day or two. They might fit *better* then, but they may never fit *well*.

Have you ever figured out why some boys buy clothes which are not entirely comfortable or do not fit really well? Quite often it is because they are set on buying a shirt or trousers of just the right color. A boy may find just the pockets and cut he is looking for. Often he does not want to admit that they are too tight or, less troublesome, too big. Because the store does not have his size and won't have it again that season, he buys some clothing which is really not right for him. There are other stores—plenty of them, as a rule.

It is best, when buying clothing, to choose from a wide assortment. Therefore, be sure to shop early in the camping season, before thousands of other campers have snapped up the best camping attire.

BEST COLORS   Soft outdoor colors are best for camp clothing. Among such colors are beige, brown, dark gray or green, and navy blue. Quiet plaids or blends of these colors are also attractive. (Lighter blues are not recommended, since they attract mosquitoes.) For a vivid touch of color, a big bandanna may be added.

BANDANNAS   Not only are bandannas fine to wear around the neck or on the head, but they have many additional uses. They can be used for carrying things, signaling, chasing flies, or making an emergency sling for an injured arm. They can also serve as sunshades and pot holders.

HATS AND CAPS   What you wear on your head in camp is pretty much up to you, though at times the weather will help decide this. A cap with a visor will keep the sun out of your eyes and the rain from running down your nose. So will a hat with a wide brim, or a rain hat. Many boys prefer no head covering at all.

RAINWEAR   What kind of rainwear to buy is one of the most difficult questions to answer. It is easy to buy rain gear which will withstand a shower or even an hour or two of rain. However, it is almost impossible to buy comfortable rainwear which will keep you really dry for longer periods.

Weatherproof coats or ponchos are better than the waterproof kind as a rule. A boy who wears a waterproof coat or poncho for an hour or so will be wet from perspiration rather than rain. The enemy will have attacked from within! A waterproof sou'wester-type oilskin with matching hat serves well in cool weather, however. Weatherproof coats or ponchos do let some rain seep through, but they cause much less perspiration. An attached hood is handy on such rainwear. To keep the legs dry, rain chaps or high rubber boots will do the trick.

In a pinch, a sheet of strong rainproof plastic can cover a camper from head to foot.

By the way, any camp clothing can be made water-repellent. Just take it to a good dry-cleaning establishment. It will spray the clothing with some weatherproofing solution such as silicone.

T-SHIRTS, PULLOVERS, AND WINDBREAKERS   A T-shirt or two and a pullover, for cool mornings and evenings, come in handy. Unlined windbreakers can be worn on cool summer days, especially in the morning and evening. Windbreakers are usually water- and wind-repellent, though not waterproof. They can be had in jacket or short coat lengths. Beige is the common color.

SLACKS AND SHORTS   Trousers should be of some close-weave, brierproof, water-resistant fabric. They should be neither waterproof nor absorbent. Hard-woven cotton, denim, chino, gabardine, and the like are best for general camp wear. They all look good. Easy-fitting jeans are also comfortable.

Cuffs should never be worn on camp slacks, because they catch on bushes, roots, and rocks, and can cause a bad fall. If you have some slacks with cuffs which are otherwise suitable for camp wear, cut the cuffs off or sew them down securely.

Shorts are good for general camp wear. They are unsuitable for bushwhacking, however.

SHIRTS   For wear around camp, everyday sport shirts are fine. But for hiking, they should be of a tough, close-weave material.

Wear long-sleeved shirts for the first few days outdoors, until you develop a protective tan. Then short sleeves give a feeling of greater freedom.

Long sleeves have one advantage over short sleeves: they can be rolled down and short sleeves cannot. This can be important when annoying insects are buzzing around.

Short sleeves should not be decorated with buttons because they are uncomfortable when you try to rest or sleep on your side.

SLEEPWEAR   Even in a rough-and-ready sort of camp, a boy should never sleep in any clothing which he has worn during the day. A clean shirt, reserved for sleeping, or ski-type night clothes or pajamas are suitable for camp. They help to assure a good night's sleep.

UNDERWEAR   Camp clothing worn next to the skin is very important. It must feel comfortable as well as be serviceable. Fortunately, today there are many wonderful space-age mixtures of fabrics which give complete comfort and wear very well. These mixtures have such trade names as dacron, nylon, and orlon. Many mixtures of wool and synthetic fabrics feel like fine-spun cotton and wear well.

For summer camp, underwear should usually be lightweight. Cotton net or even 100 per cent cotton is good, though it holds the damp and requires drying in the sun at times.

SOCKS AND STOCKINGS   Wool socks and stockings, or those made of mixtures of wool and synthetic yarns, are good for camp wear and hiking. Stockings look dressy with shorts, on visitors' day in camp, or when wearing camp clothes in town.

FOOTWEAR   The first thing to remember about any footwear worn in camp is that it must fit well and be completely comfortable. Older shoes with plenty of wear in them should be first choice. No attempt should ever be made to break in a pair of new shoes in a camp away from home. That should be done in and around the backyard camp.

A pair of stout, lightweight, ankle-high shoes is best for rough camp wear and hiking. Loafers and sneakers have their place in camp, and so have moccasins. Soft-soled footwear, however, will often cause bruises on hard ground.

Shoes worn in camp should be kept clean and lightly greased to assure long wear.

Keeping Gear in Good Condition

To get good value from his gear, a boy must not only choose it carefully, but also take good care of it.

DITTY BAG   A ditty bag helps to keep a camper's clothing in good repair. It is a little cloth or plastic bag with a drawstring, holding needles and thread, buttons, wool for darning, a few safety pins, and a small piece of beeswax for strengthening thread. Stock it to meet your own needs.

STORING TENTS BETWEEN SEASONS   Particular care must be taken when storing camp and personal gear between camping seasons. It should be dried and packed carefully. This applies to blankets, sleeping bags, tarps, and, most especially, tents. If a tent is not thoroughly dried before packing it away even for a few days, it will mildew and rot. If camp is broken up on a sunny day, the tent should be spread out and dried in the sun. If there is no sun but the day is dry, either spread the tent on the ground or hang it over lines or bushes. Complete the drying job inside the house, if necessary.

After any tent has been taken down, it should be carefully examined to see that there are no insects on the canvas. If a tent has been lying on the ground for a while, make sure that no field mouse is camping inside a fold.

When storing a tent for another season, roll it up carefully, rather than fold it. Keep it in a dry, airy place.

HOW TO AVOID LOSING IMPORTANT ITEMS Needless to say, a backyard camper cannot get full value from his gear if he loses important items soon after they are bought. It is a good idea, therefore, to tie a piece of brightly colored cloth to small objects, such as a pocketknife, compass, key ring, and the like, so that they may be easily spotted if they are dropped.

Packs

A backyard camper should learn about all aspects of outdoor life, even those which do not have immediate application in a backyard camp. He should certainly learn about packs and backpacking, in case he ever goes on a camping trip.

It is just as advantageous to rent various kinds of packs and test them in a backyard camp as it is to do the same with any other equipment. An uncomfortable pack causes no great inconvenience to a camper who doesn't have to travel far, whereas it would be a serious handicap on a camping trip. Because of this, a hike of at least five miles should be taken from the backyard camp headquarters to test the comfort and balance of any pack. A pack being tested should be full and weigh at least ten pounds but not more than fourteen.

A backyard camp is a very good place to practice packing. All things are learned best when they are not learned under pressure.

There are many kinds of good packs, each so serviceable that even experienced campers have a hard time deciding which is best. The rucksack, or knapsack, is one of the most popular packs. It has no frame and is worn on the back. The rucksack is especially suitable for canoeing and carrying personal gear and rations for an all-day hike. It is preferable to the haversack, which is made to be hung over one shoulder. Any load is more tiring when carried in this way.

Fine packs are often made from nylon or nylon-duck, because of the strength and light weight of these fabrics. Packs should be water-repellent and mildew-proof.

Lock stitching is used on the better packs. (See Chapter 2 for a description of the lock stitch.) All metal fixtures such as zippers should be rustproof. Two or three pockets on a pack are useful for stowing smaller objects which you may wish to get at easily. The best packs have a waterproof flap, to protect the contents in rain, and a double bottom.

Good pack straps or harnesses are made of leather, strong cloth, or webbing. To feel comfortable when a pack is loaded, straps should be at least one inch wide. All straps should be padded with foam rubber where they rest on the shoulders. If your pack has no such pads, sew them on.

Besides the various packs, there is the packboard, to which gear of all kinds is tied, and the pack frame, which is fitted with a pack. Modern pack frames are made of plastic and featherweight materials. They weigh less than a quarter of what they used to weigh.

The pack frame has the advantage of providing ventilation between the pack and a camper's back. The contour of a pack frame should adjust so well to a camper's back that he hardly knows that he is wearing one.

Packbaskets are still used by the Indians. The best packbaskets are made of seasoned white ash strips. Various sizes are available. These baskets are especially useful to carry small, breakable objects.

Camp Tools

In choosing camp tools, a boy should beware the danger of buying items that are flashy rather than useful. A backyard camper who likes to imagine himself cutting a path through a jungle is more apt to wind up owning a rugged-looking sheath knife, for which he will have little use, than an inconspicuous pocketknife, which has many uses. Such a boy is also likely to prefer an ax to a saw, even though a saw is likely to be far more suitable for his needs. When buying any item of equipment, ask yourself, "How much use will I have for this?" rather than "Does it look good?"

KNIVES   A good pocketknife is made of fine steel. It should have one blade about three inches long and another blade about half that length. Pocketknives with a lot of gadgets are often not as useful as they look. Such accessories are frequently too fragile to be serviceable.

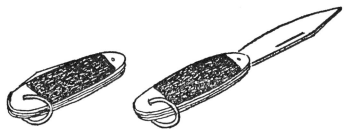

POCKETKNIFE

A jackknife, or claspknife, is a bigger sort of pocketknife. It may have one or two useful gadgets attached to it. A small screwdriver blade or a can opener can prove handy, when the knife is of good quality. The length of a jackknife usually ranges from three and a half to four and a half inches. The blade folds into the handle. Often, such knives have a ring or snap attached so they may be hung from a belt.

A bosun's knife is also serviceable. It is usually around five and a half inches long. It has one fine, functional steel blade which folds into the handle. Another useful feature is a marlin spike, for splicing and undoing tough knots. Sometimes a very short screwdriver blade is set in the opposite end from the ring or snap which attaches the knife to the belt.

Though knives are useful tools, they are also dangerous. Every camper should know how to handle them safely. By observing the following rules, a boy can avoid the most common causes of accidents with knives, and damage to them.

- Never leave a knife open or unsheathed when not in use.
- Never pass an open pocketknife to anyone. When passing a knife which does not close, hold it by the back of the blade (the dull edge) and pass it handle first.
- Never play with a knife.
- Never throw a knife, whether closed or open.
- Never drive the blade of a knife into the ground.
- Never whittle toward you, always away. When whittling, hold the knife handle tightly in your hand. Do not put a thumb on the blade. Leave enough elbow room, so that if your knife slips, it will not enter your thigh or a fellow camper.

  Never close a knife carelessly or with one hand. That is a good way to cut a finger badly. Close a knife with both hands. Keeping your fingers clear of the slot into which the blade fits, hold the knife firmly with one hand. With your fingers behind the sharp edge, carefully close the blade with your other hand, until it snaps back into the closed position.

SAWS Even in woodland or forest areas today, a saw is often far more useful than an ax. Conservation is so important that many laws prohibit cutting down saplings and bushes, especially in national and state forests and parks. A sharp saw is much better than an ax for cutting firewood into lengths. A small, lightweight coping saw or pruning saw does a better job than an ax. A buck saw is also efficient. It will prepare more firewood in a very short time than an ax will in twice the time. A folding saw or one which comes apart in sections is useful for many things besides cutting firewood. The accompanying illustration shows a bow saw of this type.

BOW SAW

AXES Despite the many restrictions placed on its use today, a small ax can still be useful. Some experienced campers use a hand ax on terrain where they are allowed to gather wood on the ground for firewood. In some national and state parks and forests, campers use axes to split logs supplied by the foresters. A hand ax can be handy in a backyard camp for driving in tent pegs and splitting pieces of wood.

If a boy knows that he will be allowed to use an ax, he should buy only a good one. A good ax is expensive but worth its price. Its blade is made of fine steel, and its well-hung handle, or helve, is usually fashioned from straight-grained hickory. It is easy to keep such an ax sharp.

The belt ax, with a 1-pound blade and a 12-inch handle, is popular with outdoorsmen. Despite its name, however, seasoned campers usually carry this ax in their pack rather than on their belt, except when in camp. Another good light ax is the Hudson Bay type. It has a 1½-pound head and a 24-inch helve.

Axes should be handled as carefully as knives. Here are some tips on handling axes safely:

- Never pass an ax carelessly. Always pass it so the handle is toward the other fellow. Don't release the blade until he has a good grip on it.
- Never leave an ax unsheathed when not in use.
- Never leave an ax lying around, even in a sheath.
- Never use a dull ax or one with a rounded blade. Such axes usually prove to be of the "tree-to-knee" variety.
- Never throw an ax for any reason.
- Never drive the blade of an ax into the earth.
- Never allow anyone within range of your ax swing.
- Never swing an ax or hammer overhead in your back-yard camp without looking to see whether there is a clothesline, wire, climbing vine, or tree branch just overhead.
- Never swing an ax or hammer with wet or sweaty hands. Handles often slip from wet hands.
- Never use an ax or hammer if the head is even slightly loose.

SHOVELS   Shovels are very handy tools and come in many forms. A shovel may be a trenching tool with a detachable handle. It may be a wood or metal scoop, or even a child's seaside spade with a sawed-off handle. This versatile tool can be used for preparation for fire-building and work around fires, ditching tents, digging latrines, and cleaning up around a tentsite. One handy shovel has a round-point blade and a 30-inch "D"-shaped handle.

BROOMS   A broom with a short, sawn-off, or detachable handle is a wonderful tool for keeping the tentsite, tent floor, kitchen, and fireplace really clean. This item is rarely found on the average camp tool checklist, despite its importance, not only as a camp tool but also as a fire-fighting weapon.

When camping in a wooded area, a camper can make a serviceable broom by lashing a dozen or more thin, supple branches found on the ground onto one end of a strong stick about two and a half feet long. Brooms also do the work of a rake in camp.

MISCELLANEOUS TOOLS   Many odds and ends which are much needed around a campsite are too often forgotten. The tools discussed here are among the most important of these, but no doubt every backyard camper will have his own necessities to add.

A pair of pliers has many uses in camp, especially one with a wire-cutting device on one side. A whetstone or flat file is handy for keeping tools sharp. Work gloves make good hand-savers, especially around the fire.

Rope, cord, and string are important in any camp. Have a length of at least fifty feet of strong rope on hand. Two lengths, one ¼-inch and the other ½-inch in diameter, are even better. Both strong cord and thinner string are indispensable.

Two coils of wire, one of # 9 gauge and the other of light wire, a few nails of assorted sizes, and a hammer round out the list of a camper's most often needed tools.

8. HAVING

FUN
with
games

A BACKYARD camper can have a lot of fun playing the games described in this chapter. Many of these games develop qualities essential for any sport—alertness, quick thinking, muscular coordination, balance, and the ability to judge distances. Some games, which are tests of knowledge, help a boy to retain the camping skills he has learned. Others are battles of wits in which one player tries to win by employing clever deception while his opponent parries with shrewd detection.

Many of these games can be played alone or with one or more friends. They come in handy for entertaining visitors or other backyard campers. Some of these games are original. Others have long been played by the American Indians. All of them require little or no equipment.

Games for Developing Physical Skills

The following games will really keep backyard campers on their toes.

BRIDGE PASS This little game can be played by two campers. It can be played in two ways. All that is required is a stretch of smooth ground and a soft rubber ball of any size, from a tennis ball to one about four inches in diameter.

One player faces the bowler and bends over with his legs apart, forming a bridge. He holds his hands just above ground level, ready to stop any bowled ball from going under the bridge.

The bowler stands ten feet away, facing the bridge. He may bowl slowly or fast, but he must bowl the ball, not throw it. The other player tries to stop it with open hands before it can roll even a little way between his legs. The bowler may pretend to bowl only once on each attempt to score a goal.

Of course, the bigger the ball, the easier it is to stop. Each goal counts three points for the bowler, and twelve to eighteen points count as a game.

BRIDGE HANDICAP PASS   This is another version of the above game. The handicap lies in the fact that the player who is the bridge stands with his *back* to the bowler. He watches the bowler and the ball from between his legs and tries to stop the ball in this position. The bowler should bowl from a distance of ten feet in this version also. The rules are the same as in "Bridge Pass."

FOOTWORK   This game is not as easy as it seems. The winners will be those boys who have the best balance. Two or more players may compete.

The players face in any direction. They start with the feet together. On the word "Go!" each player crosses his right foot over his left and turns slightly to the left, until his right toe or foot is firmly enough on the ground for his left foot to be placed directly alongside and to the left of it. Now the right foot motion is repeated and continued, always turning to the left, until each player stands in the exact position from which he started.

For the first time or so, the first player to finish without losing his balance is the winner. The game can be continued with three times around, instead of one, deciding the winner.

The game can also be played with players turning toward the right. The movements are reversed, so that the left foot is brought over the right, until the toe has enough balance to allow the right foot to be brought directly alongside it. The turning continues toward the right, until the players are back in the starting position.

In another form, the players make three complete circles as follows: one toward the left, one to the right, and the third time toward the left again. The first player around correctly wins. The changes of direction upset the balance of most players and make the game amusing for spectators.

BOWL CATCH BALL   This game and the three following games require a plastic or metal bowl and a soft rubber ball. The bowl should be about a foot in diameter and from four to six inches deep. (Smaller or larger bowls may be used, but the smaller the bowl, the more difficult the games become.) The ball may range in size from that of a tennis ball to one four inches in diameter. Games like these were favorites of the Indians.

Two players stand facing each other, about ten feet apart. One holds the bowl and the other holds the ball. The ball thrower tosses the ball slightly upward and toward the catcher, saying "Catch," as he does so. This would be very easy, but the catch is that the catcher must turn completely around once before trying to catch the ball in the bowl. The thrower *must* toss the ball when he calls "Catch," and the catcher has not much time to turn before the ball arrives.

Of course, if the ball is not thrown quite straight, the catcher may try to snare it in the bowl. If he succeeds, he earns one extra point. Each catch counts two points for the catcher, and each miss counts two points for the thrower, provided the ball has been thrown correctly. Though the ball may bounce out of the bowl, it still counts as a catch, if it does not bounce on the rim of the bowl. From eight to fourteen points counts as a game.

BOWL BOUNCE BALL   Place the bowl on level ground between two players who stand six feet away from it. Make a mark on the ground to show where each player stands. One player bounces the ball squarely into the bowl, while the other tries to catch the ball after it bounces from the bowl. Players take turns at throwing and catching.

This is not an easy game, especially for the catcher. When it is played with a tennis ball or other bouncy ball of a similar size, it is hard for even the bouncer to tell just where the ball will jump. Two points are scored for each catch, and twelve to eighteen points may count a game.

IN THREE–OUT ONE   This game and the next may be played by one or two boys. When two players contest this game, each stands six or eight feet from the bowl, which is placed on level ground in the center between the players. Marks can be made with chalk or scratched on the ground to mark each player's tossing line. The farther the tossing lines from the bowl, the more difficult the game becomes. The players take turns at tossing the ball gently, so that it lands and *stays* in the bowl.

The trick in this game is to toss the ball gently, so that it falls into and remains in the bowl. Because this is not too easy, three points are scored when the ball lands and stays in the bowl, but only one point is given when the ball lands in the bowl but bounces out. No point is scored when the ball strikes the rim or the side of the bowl without going inside. Twelve to eighteen points may be considered the game for this contest.

IN SIX—OUT THREE   The points have been increased in this version of the preceding game, since the game is much harder to play. It must be played on smooth, hard ground, so that the ball bounces well. The bowl is placed on the ground between two players. Each player stands six or eight feet from the bowl.

The stunt in this game is to bounce the ball *first* on the

ground, at any point, so that the ball rebounds into the bowl *and stays there.* Six points are scored when the ball remains in the bowl. Only three points when the ball bounces correctly into the bowl but jumps out again. Eighteen points may be counted as a game.

Games That Test Knowledge

The following games develop mental as well as physical alertness.

QUIZ BALL   This game can be played by two or more players. The quiz can cover many subjects. The only equipment is a soft rubber ball, ranging in size from a tennis ball to a volleyball.

A player (the thrower) asks a question on some subject. Then he quickly throws the ball to another player (the catcher). The catcher gives the answer as quickly as possible, while returning the ball, before the thrower counts to ten, silently and slowly.

Questions may deal with sports, movies, nature, books, history, geography, etc. When the catcher fails to answer three questions correctly, he becomes the thrower and asks the questions.

When there are several players, the thrower may throw the ball to any player, giving each a chance.

BOXING THE COMPASS   This game calls for agility, good balance, and quick thinking, besides a knowledge of the compass points, which you learned in Chapter 5. In an advanced form of this game, a player may box the compass up to sixteen points.

Mark a circle ranging in diameter from 2 to 3 feet, depending on the size of the players, on smooth, flat ground.

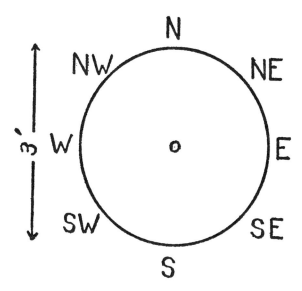

PLAYING AREA MARKED FOR BOXING THE COMPASS

Draw a smaller circle, three inches in diameter, in the center of the larger one. The big circle represents a compass, and it is marked with correctly placed compass points, as illustrated.

In its first phase, only four points (North, South, East, and West) need be marked. After the game has been played on the four cardinal points a few times, four more points may be added: Northeast, Northwest, Southeast, and Southwest.

One player is the marker. He stands on the inside circle and faces North. The other player is the caller, standing six feet away from the outer circle. The caller quickly calls any two compass points. The marker immediately jumps to place his feet on the positions called. This is easy enough to do when the points called are North and South, or East and West. However, complications in footwork arise in the second phase of the game, when eight instead of four points are in use. The caller may say "Northeast, Southwest," which is not difficult for a boy who knows sixteen compass points. But a call of "East and Southwest" demands both quick thinking and sure footwork, as the marker swings around and jumps into the correct positions. After each jump, he returns to the center circle.

When the marker makes three errors in foot-placing or loses his balance three times, the caller becomes the marker.

Guessing Games

The following games, in which each player tries to outfox his opponent, all come to us from the American Indians.

ONE-PEBBLE GAME Northwest coast Indians of all ages used to play this game for hours. The only equipment needed is a small, round pebble about three-quarters of an inch in diameter for every two players. (A marble will do.)

Two players sit facing each other. They take turns passing the pebble from hand to hand in front of them. All the while, the player with the pebble hums a tune, to try to upset his opponent's guessing ability. When the player passing the pebble is ready, he holds both hands motionless in front of him. The player doing the guessing points to the hand which he thinks holds the pebble. That hand is instantly opened. If the guess is wrong, the pebble-passer has another turn. When the guesser is right, he becomes the new pebble-passer for the next game. The Indians played this game very fast.

NONE TO FOUR This little knotting game was played by Pueblo Indian boys in the Southwest. The only gear needed is a piece of cord or thin rope about eighteen inches long.

Two boys face each other about eight feet apart. One holds the cord behind his back. When his opponent calls, "Ready," he makes any number of knots on the cord—from one to four, and perhaps none! He might tie three knots fast, so that his opponent, who is to guess the number, thinks that he has tied only one. Or he might take a minute to tie no knot at all, in the hope that the guesser will think that there must be three or four. When he is ready, he brings his empty hand in front of him.

Now the guesser states the number of knots which he believes are on the cord. Immediately the knot tier brings the cord from behind his back so the number of knots may be seen.

When two boys play this game, each player may have three chances, or the guesser may become the knotter each time he guesses correctly. The winner should be determined by the results of three or six games.

The knotter may also face three to six guessers. After the knotter has tied his knots, each guesser tells how many knots he thinks there are on the cord. After the last guesser has made his guess, the knotter brings the cord in front of him. Each boy who has guessed correctly scores one point. The first boy to guess correctly three times (not necessarily consecutively) becomes the next knotter.

MICMAC RING GAME   Two or more boys can play this game, which comes to us from the Micmac Indians. The game requires a shallow metal or plastic bowl. (A box can be used instead, but a bowl is better.) The bowl should be about eighteen inches in diameter and about three or four inches deep. A metal ring, about one and a quarter inches in diameter, is also required. A dowel, slightly pointed or rounded at one end, completes the playing equipment. The dowel should be about a foot long and three-eighths of an inch in diameter.

Fill the bowl about three-quarters full with clean sand or sawdust. The surface of the sand should be perfectly smooth.

One player takes the bowl and turns his back to his opponent. He buries the ring in the sand, not more than about an inch and a half below the surface, in any part of the bowl. He smoothes the surface thoroughly and places the bowl on a small table or on the ground.

The other player takes the dowel stick and tries to spear the ring in one try. This is not easy. (Naturally, the larger the ring and the smaller the bowl, the easier it is for the contestant to spear the ring on the first try.) The ring must be brought up on the *first* direct poke. There should be no feeling around with the stick or second poke during the first try. This automatically disqualifies the contestant, and the other takes his place.

A player who fails on the first attempt may be given a second and a third try. The ring is again buried in the sand, after each successful attempt to locate it. The best score out of three tries decides the winner.

As played by the Micmacs, this game is one of skill on the part of the player who hides the ring. When he puts the bowl down, he turns it in a certain way to fool the player with the stick into believing that the ring may be hidden toward the front of the bowl, when it is not. Or the boy who hides the ring may make one or two slight marks on the top of the sand, so the spearer imagines that the sand was displaced while the ring was being buried. This may or may not be the case.

Sometimes the Micmacs played this game in a ceremonial manner. They made quite a production out of hiding the ring and ceremoniously placing the bowl on the ground. The successful spearer became the one who hid the ring.

9. STAGING A

BACKYARD
camping
show

ONCE A BOY has developed a fair amount of skill in camp-craft, he can hold a backyard camping show and arrange displays for parents, friends, and neighbors.

Sooner or later, your parents will want to know what you have been doing and what you have learned in your backyard camp. That is the time to surprise them with a backyard campcraft show which has contests, exhibitions, and fun for everyone. Your friends will be even more surprised when they learn that it will be an audience participation event. They will have a chance to compete in campcraft games against you and perhaps other backyard campers as well.

This chapter supplies some ideas for either an afternoon or evening show or, better still, both. The evening event can be staged around a small campfire, either real or imitation. Directions for making imitation campfires are given later in this chapter.

Of course, to have a show, you must have an audience. The number of people whom you will ask to attend will naturally depend on the space available in the backyard being used. There are many ways to attract an audience. You might rely on word of mouth. However, sending out invitations, distributing flyers, and placing an eye-catching advance notice in a local newspaper will add to the excitement of the event and assure a better attendance.

If the campcraft exhibit is on a big scale, you might even charge admission. The entrance fee should be nominal. You might well decide to donate the box office "take" to some worthwhile local cause. These are things to be decided by you and any boys who are helping.

Why not treat the audience to frankfurters and hamburgers which you cook yourself? They can be cooked on a camp grill or a camp stove covered with sheet metal. Serve them on suitable buns, together with some beverage. Of course, any cooking on wood fires must be governed by local fire regulations. If wood fires are not allowed, the cooking may be done indoors.

Campcraft Exhibits

Exhibits of camping skills should be on display. The exhibition can be on a modest or large scale, depending on the amount of work you wish to put into it and whether or not the help of a few other backyard campers is available. The exhibits can be placed on improvised tables, packing cases, or even on the ground. They can include model tents and shelters, model fires, campcraft gadgetry, knots, and the like.

GADGETRY DISPLAY Models of various handy homemade camp gadgets can be made from thin dowel sticks. Or the real gadgets themselves can be displayed. If there is room in the backyard, a small tent makes a good background for a campcraft gadgetry display. Gadgets on display might include the following:

firewood carrier	tree collar
toasting forks	windbreak
wire-and-foil griddles	wash basin stand
wire-and-foil grills	Klondike blanket roll
hand guard	camp pennants
"U" grate	camp and trail signs
pot hooks	tree blazes

You learned how to make all these things in Chapters 4 and 6, remember?

KNOTCRAFT DISPLAY This display can include both the useful and the ornamental knots described in Chapter 5. Tie these knots with short lengths of fairly thick rope or sash-cord. Hang them on hooks or fasten them with adhesive tape on a thin board or sheet of heavy cardboard. The rope can be from twelve to eighteen inches long and about half an inch in diameter. One backyard camper may be in charge of this exhibit in order to explain the use of each knot and even show how the knots are tied.

A good trick effect is achieved by hanging a square knot and a thief knot side by side on a display board, with the ends of both knots covered by an inch-wide strip of paper. Someone is sure to ask why two identical knots are on display. This trick may introduce some visitors to the thief knot, which is not often seen.

A knot-tying contest is also easy to stage, as follows. The master of ceremonies requests one of the adults in the audience (preferably not a seasoned yachtsman) to compete against one of the backyard campers in knot-tying. The camper chosen should be as small as possible, but a fast and accurate knot tier. The master of ceremonies names a basic knot. Then he calls "Go." The tier who finishes correctly first wins that round. As the contest continues, the knots gradually become harder, until either the volunteer spectator has had enough or three or four knots have been tied.

CAMP AND TRAIL SIGNS   Camp and trail signs can provide a real woodsy atmosphere for a backyard camping show. They may be fastened to poles or hung on lengths of cord or clothesline, strung above adult head-level across part of the exhibition area. Tree blazes, fastened here and there with adhesive tape, can also add a colorful touch. Instructions for making these signs and blazes are given in Chapters 5 and 6.

MODEL CAMPS   One or two small models of ideal camp layouts could show a camp ready for occupancy by a lone camper or a family. The model tents can be made of pieces of strong paper or cloth of various sizes, suitably colored and held in position by small strips of adhesive tape or pasted paper. Such models can be packed flat and stored after the display. Model campfires and cook fires may be made of miniature "logs," described below.

MODEL INDIAN VILLAGE   A model of a Plains Indian village, as illustrated, can easily be set up, or a lone tepee may be used instead. Coloring the tepees in various shades adds a

MODEL INDIAN VILLAGE

pretty effect. Such model tepees are made in the same way as the model tents above. A model council fire makes this exhibit more impressive.

MODEL CAMPFIRES AND COOK FIRES   Fair-sized models of campfires and cook fires are good, easy-to-make exhibits. A camp grate, grill, and cook kit can form a part of this informative display. A collection such as this will give ideas not only to would-be and amateur campers, but possibly to a few old-timers as well.

The small "logs" used in the fire-building displays can be made most easily by painting cardboard tubes of various sizes, such as those used for mailing calendars. Logs can also be formed from stiff paper or thin cardboard. Just roll the paper up into the sizes required. Hold the model logs in shape with adhesive tape or paste sheets of brown or gray paper over them. Fold the covering and paste it over the ends of the rolls.

Suitable cardboard tubes for making large logs are harder to get. The best are those on which carpets are rolled, but such rolls are often not easy to find, though some big department stores or carpet stores may be able to supply a few. When you store the model logs for future use, slide the little ones inside the larger ones.

If local fire regulations prohibit lighting a real fire in the backyard you are using, a large model campfire can be used as the background for an evening's entertainment. Attach a 100-watt electric bulb to an extension cord long enough to reach the nearest electric outlet. Place the bulb under a dome-shaped wire frame. Cover the frame with scarlet, *fireproof* tissue paper. To add reality, paste "flames" of fireproof yellow paper onto the paper covering the dome, so that they seem to spring from the fire. Have an off-stage assistant light the fire by plugging the cord into the outlet on a word or signal from the campfire chief (probably you). The fire may be lit either before or after the audience is seated.

The spectators should be seated in a circle, whenever possible. The seating can be on benches, camp chairs, old blankets, or clean sacking borrowed from your family and neighbors. A hardy group may be content to sit on the grass, if there is any and if it is dry.

Leave soft lights burning even in the immediate campfire area, so that arriving spectators may have enough light to see clearly where they are going. Once the audience is seated, and the campfire lit, the other lights may be switched off to heighten the effect. Some additional lights may be necessary for the audience to see the performance clearly.

On with the Show!

To keep the show moving, practice being a campfire chief or master of ceremonies. Have a good program of stunts, contests, quizzes, teasers, and campfire games lined up. Each number should be suitable for all ages and require a minimum of space.

The master of ceremonies announces each event in a light-hearted way that adds to the enjoyment of the audience. He is also in charge of the songs on the program, whether solos or group singing. It is a good idea to get the audience to participate as much as possible in the show, especially if the backyard campers themselves are not too talented. The master of ceremonies should enlist the aid of any local volunteers who are able to sing or tell a few good stories.

The campfire chief and the individual performers stand beside the campfire. A flashlight, with its lit end covered by brightly colored cloth, may be used to provide a spotlight for special numbers.

A suggested program for an evening's merrymaking follows. The events are grouped under the captions, "Quizzes," "Stunts," and "Teasers." They are numbered consecutively under each category, as are the answers which are given at the end of this chapter. Thus you can have the fun of trying to figure out the answers by yourself before looking them up. No doubt you will have your own favorite quizzes, stunts, and teasers to add to the program.

Here are three types of quizzes from which to choose:

AMERICA, AMERICA

1. Where was the battle of Bunker Hill fought?
2. Name the only river in the United States which flows north.
3. Which state is bordered by only one other state?
4. Which state touches eight other states?
5. Which American president was a tailor?
6. What was President Wilson's first name?
7. Name the most northerly city in the United States.
8. Name the only American "island" which is *not* an island.
9. Which president of the United States had the largest number of children?
10. What color is the stripe at the top of the American flag: red, white, or blue?

HERE AND THERE

11. Name the Indian daughter of Powhatan.
12. Whose life did she save?
13. Whom did she marry?
14. What was the largest island in the world before Greenland was discovered?
15. Name the only walled city in North America.

THE ANIMAL WORLD

16. What is a father swan called?
17. What is a mother swan called?

18. What is a baby swan called?
19. How far can a deer run into a forest?
20. What is a baby kangaroo called?
21. What is a baby whale called?
22. What is a female fox called?
23. What would you call a beaver's home?
24. What is a baby oyster called?

Stunts

Volunteers from the audience may be asked to perform these stunts. When the campfire chief knows most of the audience quite well, he may call someone by name. If the first person to try cannot perform the stunt, someone else is called on, until the stunt has been done correctly.

These stunts can be made more amusing (provided the people called on to perform are good sports) by having each unsuccessful contestant remain beside the campfire chief until he is "rescued" by someone performing the stunt correctly. To keep the show moving, each volunteer should be given only two or three chances to do his stunt.

Many stunts can be added to those which follow. Suggested wording to introduce each stunt is given.

1. "Can you place one of your hands where the other cannot reach it?"

2. "Can you tie a knot in this piece of rope without letting go the ends?" (The campfire chief holds out a piece of rope so that volunteers can try their skill at solving the problem.)

3. "We shall pretend this invisible branch is real." (The campfire chief reaches up and puts his hands over the branch.) "Today we can swing on it by putting our hands over it and lifting our feet a little from the ground. Suppose

we return here in ten years and want to swing on this same branch. How high do you think we will have to jump to even touch this branch?"

4. "Let's pretend that you are blindfolded and I have a sack in front of me. Yes, here it is." (The campfire chief outlines the shape of the sack with pantomime.) "Inside this sack are nine white mittens and six red mittens. Please don't forget the colors. Can you tell me what is the *least possible number* you must draw out in order to have one pair of mittens of the same color?"

5. "My, we are using our imagination a lot tonight. Here we go again! Here is an empty apple barrel." (The campfire chief pantomimes.) "What can you fill it with most easily to make it lighter than it is now?"

6. Better tell your audience that the stunt which you are about to perform is called "Our Small World." Your accomplice is apparently chosen haphazardly from the audience. Ask him to go out of earshot, or have his ears tightly covered by one of the audience. In the meantime, tell the audience of your magic power. Ask the spectators to choose the name of any village, town, or city in the world and tell them that your assistant will, on his return, name the place chosen, without hesitation. The audience is surprised when he does so.

7. " 'Constantinople' is a very hard word to spell. Can *you* spell it?" (Read answer, to see how to do this.)

Teasers

Here is a sample of teasers you might use:

1. Only one sort of duck will roll on a rough lake. What species is it?
2. What two breeds of dogs would make suitable watchdogs on a spaceship?

3. What can you hold in your right hand that you can't hold in your left?
4. Why is a skunk in a tent like a house afire?
5. If a father gave one of his sons fifteen cents and the other ten cents, what time would it be?
6. What will be yesterday, although it was tomorrow?

Answers

Now let's see how well you have been able to figure out the answers and solutions to the quizzes, stunts, and teasers for yourself.

QUIZ ANSWERS

1. On Breed's Hill, a quarter of a mile from Bunker Hill.
2. The Saint John's River. It flows north from Lake George, past Jacksonville, Florida, to the Atlantic Ocean.
3. Maine.
4. Tennessee.
5. Andrew Johnson.
6. Thomas.
7. Fairbanks, Alaska.
8. Rhode Island.
9. William H. Harrison.
10. Red. There are seven red and six white.
11. Pocahontas.
12. Captain John Smith.
13. John Rolfe.
14. Greenland.
15. Quebec.
16. Cob.
17. Pen.
18. Cygnet.

19. Halfway. Once that mark is passed, the deer is running out.
20. Joey.
21. Calf.
22. Vixen.
23. Lodge.
24. Set.

STUNT ANSWERS

1. One hand placed on the elbow cannot be touched by the other hand.

2. When a person's arms are folded across his chest *before* he takes up one end of a rope in each hand, the knot will be made as his arms are unfolded.

3. *No* jump is required. A tree grows from the top, so the branch will still be at the same height in ten years.

4. Drawing out three mittens will do the trick. By luck it can be done by drawing out two mittens, but one cannot depend on that.

5. Holes.

6. Your accomplice knows in advance that any place mentioned immediately after a city or town consisting of two words is the place chosen by the audience. He promptly says "That's the one" or "That's it," after you call any name following a city or town such as San Francisco, New Orleans, Baton Rouge, Hong Kong, or New York.

Of course, you must be alert to stage this trick correctly. You should name at least six places in different parts of the United States or the world in general before naming any city with a two-word name. If you name any town or city with a double name unintentionally, you will cause your helper to give a wrong answer. Concentrate on the fact that your helper is going to select the city *immediately after* the first two-word place-name called by you. Practice this stunt together to be sure that it will work smoothly.

7. This is an old spelling stunt that still works today. In the old days, the person questioned won by spelling "it," which is what he was actually asked to do. Today there is a modern twist to this "catch." It is a test of your cleverness, matched against the person whom you are trying to catch.

Have your victim come forward. Then say, "You may not think that 'Constantinople' is a hard word to spell, but it really is. To make it easier for you, I am going to pronounce the word in syllables. Even if you can spell it that way, you are a top speller. Now, try: Con- (pause, while he spells it), stan- (pause), ti- (pause), no- (pause)."

If you are really cagey about the way you say "no," immediately after the contestant has spelled "ti" correctly, he will think that he has spelled "ti" incorrectly. So will many of the audience. He may suggest "te." Even if he repeats "ti," you will probably discourage him by saying "no" again emphatically. He will probably retire puzzled, leaving you to try your skill on another victim. Eventually, somebody may spell "no" right after "ti." If this happens, you lose. Of course, you must acknowledge that the contestant has spelled the word correctly.

This is a mean catch. Skillful voice inflection may add several victims to your credit before someone catches on!

ANSWERS TO TEASERS

1. A wooden or plastic decoy. No real duck rolls.
2. Airdales and Skye Terriers.
3. The left elbow.
4. The sooner it is put out, the better.
5. Twenty-five to two.
6. Today.

Sources of Camping Information

Boys who have learned the camping skills explained in this book may someday wish to camp farther afield. Here are some good sources of information on federal, state, and private campsites.

For information about the national parks of the United States, write to the Superintendent of Documents, Government Printing Office, Washington, D.C. 20402 for a free, complete list of pamphlets on the subject, entitled *National Parks, Historic Sites, and National Monuments.* The list gives the price of each pamphlet, which usually runs from 5¢ to 20¢. If you prefer, write to the National Park Service, Department of the Interior, Washington, D.C.

To find out about campsites in our national forests, write to U.S. Forest Service, Department of Agriculture, Washington, D.C. You can also write to the Superintendent of Documents, Government Printing Office, Washington, D.C. 20402 for the booklet *National Forest Vacations.* Enclose 30¢. Send 20¢ to the Superintendent of Documents for the pamphlet *America's Playgrounds.*

For information about state parks, write the director of state parks or the department of conservation in the capital of the state in which you wish to camp. For information regarding campsites in state forests, write the state forestry department in the capital of the state where you plan to camp.

Other sources of campsite information are the Bureau of Outdoor Recreation, Washington, D.C. 20240 and American Youth Hostels, 20 West 17th Street, New York, N.Y. 10011. Chambers of commerce are usually glad to provide information about camping facilities in their areas.

The Backyard Camper's Code

I pledge ●●●●●●●●●●●●●●●●●●

- *never* to mark walls with paint or chalk or in any other way that cannot be easily washed off when the purpose of the marks is accomplished.
- *never* to cut or otherwise injure trees, bushes, plants, or flowers.
- *never* to dig holes in the ground without first getting permission to do so.
- *never* to leave any odd gear lying on the ground or on benches.

●●●●●●●●●●●●

I promise ●●●●●●●●●●●●●●●●●●●

- *always* to keep my camp clean, tidy, and shipshape.
- *always* to store gear out of sight when not in use.
- *always* to take good care of my equipment and gear.
- *always* to observe all those city, suburban, or rural regulations regarding fires and other things which pertain to my camp and activities in it.
- *always* to practice all of the safety pointers given in this book.
- *always* to safeguard my health and that of other people by observing all health and sanitation requirements.
- *always* to be sure that any ropes or wires which must be strung across the campsite are well above adult head-level.
- *always* to be patient and courteous when visitors inquire about my progress as a camper.
- *always* to observe camper courtesies and respect the rights of others.

SIGN YOUR NAME HERE

The Backyard Camper's Code—155

index